PROFILE OF LOVE & COURAGE

SECOND SPRING PART II

Elmer Abear, MD
and
Cesar Abear, AB

authorHOUSE®

AuthorHouse™
1663 Liberty Drive
Bloomington, IN 47403
www.authorhouse.com
Phone: 833-262-8899

Published by AuthorHouse 07/15/2022

ISBN: 978-1-6655-6409-0 (sc)
ISBN: 978-1-6655-6407-6 (hc)
ISBN: 978-1-6655-6408-3 (e)

DEDICATION

Bishop Terry R. La Valley, J.C.L.
Bishop of Ogdensburg, N.Y.
New York, U.S.A.

PREFACE

Another book of sharing the faith and poignant memories of childhood and beloved City of Argao, Cebu in the Philippines. In this book, the author, Elmer Abear, touches on science in relation to faith.

Passed down stories of past generations of the Abear clan and their early life in his eyes growing in Argao. The book also touches on politics up until BLM and Covid 19 lockdown. All of these are in short stories for the reader to take breaks and ponder about the subjects. There are a few articles that I contributed about faith, work and giving. The last part in this book is a collection of poems penned by the author Elmer. The poems express the deep poetic emotions of his soul. So, I wish you a happy read.

By SOE (Son on Earth)

CONTENTS

POEMS

ARTICLES

THE 3RD EYE

Of your body & soul

THE "MYSTERY"
OF THE PINEAL GLAND

GLAND

The article is only a tip of the iceberg of what the 3rd eye is all about with regards to your body and soul. Anatomically, the Pineal Gland, an endocrine gland (1), is located at the center of the brain.

It joins the 2 halves of the thalamus (2). It secretes Melatonin, a sleeping hormone that influences our sleep patterns, abundant when sleeping and reduced by the presence of light (3).

The lack of this hormone when you are supposed to sleep causes fatigue and tiredness; a higher level during waking hours and drinking too much coffee or any stimulants may cause insomnia (4).

Most if not all vertebrates have pineal gland. To mention one without we have the Alligator (5). Therefore, it is conceivable that this particular animal lacks compassion.

People who lack compassion are primarily like an Alligator: Quiet under water but deceptive, fierce, and brutal if opportunities are opened before him. On the hindsight, they are less dangerous than the ISIS.

For example, when an Alligator is resting on the sand, he keeps his big mouth. He knows he has the best food it could offer to flies. Once his mouth is filled with flies, though he pretends he is sleeping he would suddenly close his mouth and bang! Gourmet food! Heh, heh.

Good, delicious food: if you look at the Alligator's eyes: he smiles. Most of them are taken in, lucky are those who were able to escape. If you do not call that deceptive, lack of compassion, greedy, and cruel, I don't know what is. So, you remember if some people are like that - alligators in human form, heh, heh. Be Careful. You could be taken without your awareness, like flies.

Ironically, some people act this way, deceptive, greedy, showing compassion like an Alligator for satisfaction of their greed. Sad to say there are numerous people like this in any government in the world. Plenty of Alligators!

Thanks God, Fox News exposes thru O Reilly's program so that among the morally right people it keeps his show for 12 years No. 1 at the writing. Nevertheless, some media like an Alligator either justify their moral relativism or ignore it for their own "aberrant" satisfaction.

What can you and I say about them? We can say it is "conceivable" that their pineal gland is "calcified" or hardened and the AMTP which is an enzyme that destroys pathological cells (6) may have been inhibited or simply the lack of it.

The combination of the physical and spiritual within the cell we can safely say, 'it is the 'corporal work of mercy.' The cell is like an empty car waiting for the passengers of ideas.

Hence you and I are no mere matter as Atheist would think but we are creatures of God, the father, saved by Christ and provided a conscience and free will (the essence of love) by the Holy Spirit.

THE 3rd EYE

"Know thyself" is the famous legacy of Socrates before Christ. Whether you believe it or not, to know more of yourself is to know more about the spiritually of the pineal gland. Which R. Descartes refers to it as the "principle of the soul" and views it as "the third eye." (7)

He further posits the idea in respect of those who find the inconclusive eye of the soul and says," it is a link between the intellect and the body." It is God's gift to all of us.

Just as your body has two eyes that you may see 'one' at a time, you also have the 3rd eye, you may see one in three aspects of the 3rd eye:

1. FREE WILL:

In triune (likes God's divine trinity), you see one God in three divine persons. Unfortunately, because of your FREE WILL you and I either choose to know or ignore it for good. Does it benefit anyone to know the spiritual functions of the 3rd eye of the soul?

Your answer is probably "Yes." For Yes opens your 3rd eye thru meditation to the mystery of yourself and beyond. Read the "Power of Positive Thinking" to complement its scientific know-how and you will perhaps have clearer evidence of the mystery of the 3rd eye, not to mention the writing of the Holy Spirit thru Thomas E. Kempis based on God's own word, the Holy bible.

What about if you ignore our 3rd eye? You might widen your vista in the world around you at the expense of the vision of the 3rd eye. Does it not contradict the fact that as I said we see a triune and now it seems we see one in two?

You could be right if I did not mention the gift of FREE WILL in which I repeat: the right to choose between good and evil. You don't actually see one in two, you still see a triune. But a triune that is not divine. Got it?

Just as you have the 3rd eye of the good soul which makes you and I "God's image and likeness," the heavenly Father of Truth, you could also have an "image and likeness of Lucifer" the light in darkness we call, "Father of lies." It seems God is "fair and balanced" to Lucifer, is not it.

3

Hence, if you are a liar like the 2014 President of the USA who allegedly lied 253 times (source FOX news) then he earned the honor as a child of Satan, Father of Hell. I am not sorry to say that. Neither do I rejoice what I mean. I pray.

For I was there myself, a slave of Lucifer for a long time until I began to know the truth, much more so the information I got from the 3rd eye fixed on Christ. Humbly, the truth sets me free.

In a sense, you seem to have a power more than God and more than Lucifer because through your subtle manipulation you have both gifts, good and evil. Naturally, you reduce truth to an idea that is relative and with a lie. Moral relativism creeps into your hide and is America responsible for the increase of crimes?

Neither God or Lucifer, through God allows it, does not essentially have "moral relativism" because they would like to win your soul and mine absolutely. No room for compromise. Satan is not a relative. It may be used as a trap for one's absolute end.

At the end of time, there is no more purgatory. We had so much while on earth. Hence, you and I may either go to Hell or Heaven forever. During this glorious time when we have our body back and soul together.

We say this every time we pray the CREED, "The resurrection of the body and life everlasting." If you do the Greek word, "diabolus."

It is interesting to note that when our body and soul are joined together at the end of the day of Resurrection which Jesus promised us (he set an example himself when his body and soul were together at the Resurrection) we will look as handsome as we were on earth at age 16.

Proof: when our Mother Mary died at the age of 70, she appeared in Fatima with her body and soul as young as 16 years old. Our Mother Mary was not subject to moral decay of the body because she was born free from original sin.

How could God, this is Jesus, being the womb <u>stained with original sin?</u> Hence, she said it herself before St. Bernadette when asked who she was, and she answered: <u>"I Am the Immaculate Conception."</u>

In conclusion, when some of us would recite the CREDO, it would no longer be a lip service but a reality for Christ who said: <u>"I am the way, the truth and the life."</u>

Warning: If you don't believe in Hell (like you won't believe in the resurrection of the body) let me say what Padre Pio said to a non-believer: <u>"You will believe in Hell once you will be there."</u>

2. CONSCIENCE:

Whether you can choose good or evil, God, not the devil has given you a gift that you do not own. You and I call it <u>"conscience." To start with: no one owns his/her conscience.</u> Conscience is the ability to know what is right or wrong. Science is a gift you can either lose or keep it for good.

For example, after a killer murdered several people (too many examples to mention) he could not handle his good conscience, so he took his own life. If he owned it, he could have just ignored it. This is to differentiate from a pathological liar where his/her conscience is dead.

Two examples of dead conscience out of many, Hitler and Marcos, the Philippines dictator in the 70's where more than 100 thousand Filipinos died a cruel death. Two examples of good conscience out of many, Thomas More and Benigno Aquino, Sr.

So, if you often play by that rule, which makes you neither good nor bad, you subject yourself to what God of Truth says that each of our decisions is subject to judgment at the end of our life. <u>Heaven is absolute truth and so is Hell.</u>

Hence, the fall of Adam and Eve, our first parents, becomes a reality to recon with for a better understanding of you and me. It is not therefore

5

hard for you to understand that if we constantly ignore the 3rd good eye, we strive more for material successes than spiritual.

You see what you believe. In this process you inhibit yourself from the beauty and grandeur of the spiritual world beyond us. Why? In most instances you and I are afraid to change our lifestyle.

What is tragic you nevertheless would arrive at the end of your life into the world of spirits which in reality is life forever, leaving behind a world what Alfred Tennyson would say, "life is only a dream." So far so clear?

Let us review further our understanding of the 3rd eye. The 3rd eye, I repeat, is the Pineal gland situated at the center of the brain. Our entire brain is floating on a fluid called cerebrospinal fluid which is connected to 12 nerves that comprise the movement and thinking of our senses. This CSF also bathes the entire con shape Pineal gland.

Almost everything that enters the brain comes from your seven senses. You therefore learn from your senses. Anything beyond the senses is a mystery to recon with. Here the 3rd eye plays an important role.

Anyway, as I said the Pineal Gland is a cone shaped, facing the center of our brain called the "midbrain." Those who choose to develop this 3rd eye called it "the seat of the soul" must know the spiritual "tools" how to do it. Religious belief may vary but most of the time the "tools" for spiritual perfection is practically the same. Praise the lord.

Let us take for example - Socrates. Socrates apparently not know God the father thru Christ's revelation discovered that man was not only a composite of matter but had a soul. His defense led him to his death. Socrates was an honest man. He had only one request before he was given a poison to drink that he had forgotten to pay a check for his neighbor: he asked that he pay. It was fulfilled.

Anyway, those who choose to ignore it particularly are Atheist and Skeptics and I do not know what they call it. On scientific ground the

Pineal Gland is an endocrine gland and has several functions but few if any is known about "it" (the soul).

The Pineal gland thru its pinealocytes secretes an enzyme called Melatonin. Which at birth, a scientist discovered was abundant in the first 2 years of life. Its high amount has been suspected to inhibit sexual desires (5). Hence, this age is considered the "age of innocence."

If its level is higher before the age of puberty it would cause precocious puberty resulting in a large sexual organ (usually people of large private parts appear less intelligent) which does not necessarily translate to increased libido. If you don't believe it, ask those who are "lucky" to have big sexual organs. It is the pride and plum of the few. Most love "Cialis."

Anyways, at puberty when it is few, it activates the hormone part testosterone which drives a lot of young people (including me when I was a teenager) crazier and did not know what to do to calm it down. Ice packed, heh heh. Otherwise, you know what I mean.

However, there are people who could express their purity of mind of inhibition for the love of God and one out of many I could think of is Saint Padre Pio who used to play with angels at the age of innocence.

So, when Padre Pio greeted his classmates and asked if they had played with their angels, they looked at him as "weirdo." So, Padre Pio never spoke about his encounter with angels. Hence in general, one who strives to be closer to God and has spiritual encounters are most often considered "different."

Of course, those who played with the devils were many and to mention one out of the few chosen devils you have is Bishop of Hippo, St. Augustine who fathered several children out of wedlock, not to mention St. Mary Magdalene, the high-class prostitute whom the Elite allowed to enter to see Jesus in their holy place.

How did each become a saint, not by Augustine's own merit but through the merit of their mother, St. Monica who prayed for him for about 20 years. It is very important that we pray for others, if you save a soul, all your material successes are nothing compared to the fact that you are assured of heaven for yourself.

Before we proceed further, it might be more worthy to mention a Saint who appeared a slave to promiscuity. Who is this guy, do you know? This guy is St. Francis of Assisi who was reminded by the devil the pleasure of fornication he gave up.

God allowed the devil to tempt him day and night for 6 months about fornication of all sorts that he got so healthy angry that he rolled his body in the garden of roses and as a result all the thorns went into his body. And from there on he was promised by God that he would possess the "purity of the mind." NOTE: Don't try it.

My wife and I personally saw and touched this vine of roses without thorns in front of St. Francis' statue which at that time a white dove symbolically was in his arms.

That's a couple of examples of saints who developed their 3rd eye to the fullest. How did they do it. Simple. Meditate and obey the 10 commandments given by God to Moses. You can do this when you love God above all things.

And to make it simple and easier for the mind to remember Jesus reduced it to 2 commandments: "Thou shalt love God above all things and love your neighbor as you love yourself."

Love your neighbor as you love yourself in the first of the three steps to perfect holiness. You see, if you love your neighbor like the way, you love yourself you have not completely denied yourself for the love of God. I could be wrong please correct me.

The 2ⁿᵈ step is to love your neighbor as Jesus said, "<u>deny yourself</u>." For example, you have a very beautiful car, but you deny yourself and sacrifice it to your only daughter for her to use in school.

The 3ʳᵈ step is to "<u>love your neighbor and forget yourself</u>." This is a true example: a man jumped to save a drowning child and was able to save the child but lost his own life. Very often the last 3ʳᵈ step is your door to Heaven like all Christian who faced martyrdom for their faith. One of many examples: St. Thomas More.

THE WILDFIRE OF PAPA ANOY

As a little house boy of a rich man in Argao, Anoy used to tip toe by the window looking at boys & girls of his age laughing & joking with each other's on their way to school nearby.

How he wished to go to school but the rich man won't allow him. He would say to him, "You're my Alipin (slave). Alipin don't go to school."

He was found one time eating on the table with his children and he got shouted, "Alipin, don't eat on the table. You go down and wait until we are done." Anoy would just go down & wait in the corner till they were done and ate what was left on the table.

While eating their dog came nearer to him. Anoy could not stand his pleading eyes asking for food. He shared his food to the dog and went to bed & felt hungry on behalf of his dog. Nearby his dog slept well like a contented cow.

That was decades ago. He was now married to Siana Espina. For his livelihood he was a fisherman like the 12 Apostles of Christ. After a night of fishing people would gather at the seashore in Tulic to buy his fish.

On one occasion he did not catch enough fish and after keeping a fish for Siana to cook, a man approached him. He had no money to buy and needed some for his hungry family.

Anoy became emotional & he could not refuse anyone who asked. That was his character, to give until it hurt. So, he gave his only fish. Upon arriving home, Siana was asking for a fish to cook.

Anoy said, "Here is money buy a sardine for our dinner." Anoy had a very understanding wife. They had sardine for dinner that night.

At one time while cleaning His net for an evening fishing he saw 3 big burly boys mocking an old man in tattered short with His private between His thighs.

Anoy could not stand the abuse and the humiliation the old man suffered. He told them to stop bullying but they instead positioning for a fight.

Little did they knew he was judo expert. As each of them threw a punch Anoy threw them one by one far away into the deep sea.

His generosity and courage spread like wildfire across many towns. And because of his generosity and kindness with strength people called him, "Papa Anoy," meaning, their father in town.

So that when the town held their first election for Mayor, though he personally did not like to run against a school's supervisor as his opponent he could not say, no. He was a positive man for whatever he could do for his neighbors or anyone for that matter.

On debate the Supervisor said to the people, "Don't vote for Anoy because he is "*ignoy*" meaning ignorant. Anoy would counter-attack and humbly say, "He is right!" (He made no excuses of his poverty).

And so, he said, "Vote for him. I'm not educated like him." He always faced the naked truth for what he honestly was. When the vote was counted Papa Anoy won by land slide. The Supervisor left town. One Summer in July 2001 I left New York to Argao and visited the Municipal bldg. I saw a long line up of pictures of Mayors.

I walked to the very end. And at the end I saw the name of the first Mayor: Mariano E. Abear, the only Mayor who had no photo of himself.

Per chance I visited. My niece, Elizabeth and found an old album: the family of Papa Anoy, surrounded by 9 of his children, in front were my little brothers & his cousins, the Minozas & the Montenegros.

I instructed Elizabeth to get the best Artist in Cebu City to create a picture of him. All expenses charged to me. I emailed to her until now I've not received a response from her. She is excused because she is a busy woman. I hope I can do this myself. Amen.

THE PRAYER OF UNCLE PASCIO

This is a true story of Uncle Pascio, of what I thought of his beliefs in comparison with mine and perhaps with yours too.

Maybe, out of our differences, we might be able to sort it out what we might have missed as to how to live a happier life, especially in the pursuit of happiness, which nothing seems to satisfy us.

Well, after Uncle Pascio graduated Valedictorian in Grade VI, in Argao, Cebu, he eloped Nang Soling, his elderly Father's helper at home.

Fearing the anger of the helper's father he fled to Mindanao. In a small town where he become a farmer and also served for a period of time in his community as a Barrio Captain or Counselor. Otherwise, he would have remained as an ordinary farmer of the town.

After several decades, he moved and eventually settled in Binugao, Davao City. He encouraged my father to buy lots in the area and promised to protect the property from any Muslims who might steal coconuts or banana fruits.

Indeed, he fulfilled what he promised. So, whenever some Muslims would attempt to steal coconuts or other fruits in our land, he would fight them with his unbelievable karate-judo or if not face his home made-gun.

The Muslims never ventured into our farm until the day he died at age 90+ due to natural death in his nipa-house.

During those days when he was alive, he did not like me that much. But I, as a doctor, tried to take care of his health whenever he needed my help. Free of charge.

I prescribed no pills except lotion to help him from too much itchiness of his dry skin. He made it worse by rubbing alcohol on his skin.

The last time I visited him I noticed his feet were bare. I thought of buying him a pair of shoes. But, on the second thought nature had provided him a thick callous on both feet to plow his rice field or dry cornfield. Shoes were obviously irrelevant.

I bought him a Barong Tagalog to attend my parent's Golden Wedding in 1964. He attended but he did not wear the Barong Tagalog. Instead, he wore an appropriate white long sleeve shirt. He looked descent.

I always wondered why he seemed not to like me that much, but even with that I loved him more. I'm not a masochist. What drawn me to him was his simple life that I still do not have. Uncle Pascio was about 132 lbs., 5'7" tall but very strong thin-chested man & feared no one.

Meanwhile, I pray that I would still be alive "at the end of time." I knew it was a silly prayer, but I pray mainly to remind him, you & our future generations to prepare what Jesus said at the end of time,

"He will wipe away every tear from their eyes, and death shall be no more, neither shall there be mourning nor crying nor pain any more, for the former things have passed away." (Revelations 21:4) There will be the resurrection of the body & soul... I will come to judge, the living & the dead" (Nicene Creed).

Which means, no more Purgatory but only Hell & Heaven. Can you imagine how painful it would be to be in Hell with our own body & soul? And to be forever at that. I planned to ask Uncle Pascio if he believed in God.

Whether you believe or not in "the end of time" it will happen anyway. Life, indeed, is forever for what we choose at the end of time, Heaven or Hell. Do not forget that my friend!

Meanwhile, Pascio lived by his conscience, what God has endowed every creature, whether they are white, brown, black, or yellow, a colorless soul to handle His gift of good will & conscience, which some of us are incapable of.

For God's love is something that no man can fathom or understand like a dog to a man's intelligence. Sometime some people think and act like animals, which make a dog or cat a better friend.

I cannot understand why some people eat black dog in some 3rd world countries. I tasted one not knowing it was a dog's meat. It tasted very good. When I knew it: I felt like throwing up.

Anyway, Uncle Pascio who followed his conscience which told him the choice to do good & avoid evil. When he did to do good & avoid evil became a habit forming it was a lot easier to do good & avoid evil.

I tried that but it did not work. Uncle Pascio practiced what he believed. Good for him. Anyway, those who do the opposite they lost their consciences and won't hesitate to do evil than good.

Scripture says, these are "evils in human forms." To mention a few, they are the liars and to mention a few they foment abortion, chaos, violence, murders, and same sex marriage.

One day, I asked Uncle Pascio if he believed in God. He said, "Elmer, I only say to God every morning, thank you for giving me another day." And that was it.

And he worked almost all the days of his life, staying behind his Carabao to support his family. Never heard him complaining about his life as some of us would do, including myself.

His sport was to go to "*Sabongan*" & bring his Texas fighting cock. Though seldom he lost, I liked it whenever he did. His dead Texas cock becomes my favorite "*sinabaw nga manok*", my favorite especially mixed with "*Camonkgay*." Oh boy, just to think of it, *nag ta bisay ang akong laway.*

What was awesome about Uncle Pascio: he was very honest & sincere in his life. You could not cross that line, or you would be in trouble with him.

Uncle Pascio was just like my own Father, Juan. I'm still struggling to imitate their "old" values to avoid my new vices. Those who know me understand that. Pray for me.

I think God took care of Uncle Pascio. He might not have the Sanctifying Grace I have after every good confession to Christ in "Persona Christi," but God's divine mercy is available from Jesus thru St. Faustina every 3 PM at EWTN, a global network.

Remember what Christ said on the cross to a thief from his right side? "Father, forgive them; for they know not what they do." (Luke 23:34)

This thief went to paradise with Christ. For a 3 day stop over near Hell he wore with mask over his snot nose because the odor of Hell was unbearable, while Christ "descended into Hell & on the third day He rose again to Heaven." (Nicene Creed). What Christ said on the cross, Uncle Pascio might not know what he was doing for example, not going to Mass on Sundays.

How blessed it is for one who does not honestly know what he is doing; his opportunity to go to Heaven is greater than most of us who know Christ's two "greatest commandment" (Matthew 22:24-40).

Later, his daughter sent me a picture, showing Uncle Pascio seemingly to have a smile on his face in his inexpensive coffin. He wore the Barong Tagalog I gave him & on his feet a new pair of shoes.

MADE IN CHINA

When I was taking my Ob-gyn residency in 1978 at the University of Newfoundland, I was accommodated in an apartment just at the back of St. Mary's Hospital.

Somebody was knocking at my door in this early morning. I opened the door & here came a scholar from China in her 50's.

She bowed & said, "Good morning" and I answered, "Welcome home." I don't remember if I bowed. I should have done that. Anyway, when she saw a Crucifix of Christ crucified, she was trembling & horrified and exclaimed, "What has he done?"

I was amazed & surprised. Word was beyond my lips to answer. If you were in my position, I doubt if you can find a word to explain. I just thought, "her soul was created by God, but her body was made in China."

We had coffee & bread for our breakfast. I cannot remember her name. She must be a brilliant Doctor sent by the Chinese Govt. to study further on Cardiology-medicine.

China is a rich Nation (that threatens USA). If most Leaders & some people do not know God I wonder if after life they can enter the gate of Heaven which Jesus said,

"It easier for a Camel to pass thru the eye of a needle than a rich man to enter the gate of Heaven" (Matthew 19: 24). Be happy, if the eye of your needle is bigger than your Camel.

After our pleasant conversations we parted sweet goodbyes. There was no mentioned about the crucified Christ. I had in my room a Crucifix.

I held my Crucifix & kissed Jesus, an Adilene collection & at its back written, Made in China.

I remembered the word of Christ from the cross, "Father, forgive them (China) for they do not know what they are doing" (Luke 23: 34). Good for them than what little I know. Heaven for me is not easy than that Doctor made in China.

OF CHURCH & CAESAR

The Supreme Court of America decided constitutionally not to limit the number of people worshiping inside the Churches or Synagogues.

However, our good Governor of New York, using Covid-19, to restrict freedom of Religion ordered - "that only 10 people to worship inside the Church".

However, God, in alter Christus was asked by the Pharisees the role between Church & Caesar (Govt) Christ said: "Give to Caesar what belongs to Caesar and give to Church what belongs to Church" (Mark 12: 13-17).

The Pharisees were astonished of His wisdom but unlike the Governor of New York, it appeared he was questioning the minds of the 5 best legal minds of America.

Due probably to lack of faith the Governor did not realize that like a coin having 2 sides (like husband & wife) it is supposed to work side by side for the love of the Governor's neighbor. Remember, the 2nd greatest commandment of Christ, "Love your neighbor the way you love yourself." (Matthew 22:39)

To expand our insight into this restriction Joseph & Mary traveled from Nazareth to Judea in spite of Mary was 9 months pregnant, "to render to Caesar what belongs to Caesar".

This seems like the same decree by the Govt. of America that all Americans should wear mask during this Pandemic to prevent this Covid-19 virus from spreading.

This Corona virus was not created in Wuhan Lab, China. It is therefore naive to blame China. Dr. Fauci, a Scientist, 2nd to none said that this virus sprang from nature.

I cannot rule out when one step more he might have known it was created by a murderer called, the Prince of Darkness allowed by God, almighty, Creator of Heaven & earth to chastise the world.

This event in our 20th century like the plague during George Washington time in 1837 which drove him to emigrate to America.

He founded a Govt of the people with indispensable Constitution UNDER GOD that this Nation be protected against the Leftist agenda which it appears no doubt against God.

Poor Joseph must have had emptied his saving to buy a Donkey for Jesus, a 9-month-old baby in the womb of Mary to ride for weeks on end of travel to register in Judea.

Joseph knew Mary was carrying the Messiah, promised by God in his dream. They tried to ask along the way for a night's shelter because Mary had on & off uterine pain in Bethlehem late in the evening of December 24 (Luke 2:1-7).

They pleaded from house to house, seeing them, carrying 2 doves unlike the rich with their goats they were refused.

Mind you, it was not the will of God but the will of man that drove Joseph, Baby Jesus in the womb of Mary homeless and ended up Jesus being born in a manger. Can you believe that?

If I were Joseph in a healthy arrogance I would have said, "Look I am carrying God in the womb of my (bethrown) wife who is the Messiah, promised by God in my dream."

What a big laugh & sneer I would have received (if you there and said no doubt). "Out you go away & dream some more!"

Today, with this restriction to limit to 10 my big family & numerous friends "to render to God what belongs to God", have affected us

Our good Governor of New York allowed people to buy liquor, marijuana & open bar & eat in restaurants but shutters Churches & Synagogues. If this is not hypocrisy, tell me what it is that I may find peace in my soul.

Oh, How I missed to receive "the Body of Christ that saved me, to drink His blood for the forgiveness of my sins, his passion to strengthen me" (Anima Christi) of my cowardice. Oh, Lord, not by your judgement but with your divine mercy, I commend my spirit. Amen.

OF DOGS & PANDEMONIUM

Part I

For your entertainment let us talk about some people who will see their souls in relationship with either God, Satan & the "I, me, & myself."

20% of young people in New York did not find God during lockdown in their souls or to be fair with Satan and instead seeing their egos they took their lives away.

Lives did not matter to them: Black lives mattered to them. May they rest in peace. BLM do not unfortunately entertain some people.

Their goal is a rebirth of Marxism which Germany & Russia had rejected decades ago. They found nothing in it but death & persecution of the people.

Cowards like some football players who seem not to know more than what their feet can kick, or hands can catch, they are supposed to entertain the public in general. Not party affiliated as they appear to be rather than what they should be what they are.

However, majority of people are probably in and out of considering between Heaven & Hell. Well, for us who still survive let us have some fun from nature, out of which God has created Pets like Dogs as man's best friend.

And surely find the difference between man's intelligence & dog. Dog never question that difference because dogs might think that God has created him/her unlike human being, a perfect creature naked like Adam & Eve before the fall into the hand of Lucifer.

We cloth dogs because we inherited the shame of Adam & Eve. If some people think that is a myth, then try to walk naked like, St. Francis of Assisi who suddenly was free of sin.

Ashamed of his nakedness a Bishop allegedly removed his extra brown apparel and covered St. Francis to remind him that he is one of us.

Maybe that might explain most Franciscans wear brown clothes. I wonder if under (excuse me) their brown, "sotana" they had T shirts, not to mention briefs.

Perhaps like St. Francis of Assisi with stigmata looking at Jesus half naked on the cross they might consider, free of sin. I'm sorry if I sound vulgar in my language. Forgive me. I'm just curious like Eve, taking my reputation if there is little at risk.

Well, to go further into this insight, for the first time in decades at age 83 I had decided to go jogging (not naked) walking like legged old ducks with my naked dog.

I was looking at the sky or scanning the green landscapes for Ground Hog & dry trees, swinging in the wind for rain with my best friend, a teenage dog named, Potsie.

This teenage, spoiled brat went with me jogging always ahead of me as if he knew the way, the truth & the life of a dressed man like me.

Anyway, whenever he stopped, I had to pull him up so that he had no time to pick up prime grass to eat or pooh from Ducks.

When I was halfway (my usual 30 minutes) jogging Postsie put on his hard break. We stopped & he poohed. You know what he would do, smelled his urine & then ate his pooh. Do you know? He had recycled his own waste matter.

Mom said to me. I did the same thing, eating my pooh flavored with urine when I was 3-4 months old. I was no better than a doggy. I was an innocent animal. Naive might be a softer word since I happened to be a human little baby.

When we reached home, I put Potsie free into the sala. When he saw me: with Happy, a dog equivalent to an old 80 yrs. woman, was in my loving arms Potsie got furious & wanted to go with us.

I told him, "No, Sir! You are done." And he turned away. I supposed he understood & jumped on the sofa with disappointed eyes. I could not care less I had to be fair with Happy.

I did not do any jogging with an 80-year-old who happened to be at the same age with me. We instead walked like two old four legged ducks. Happy was excited: He hopped & jumped.

Then, she made her water. I knew because her tail was way down between her legs. If her tail would be up, she would make a pooh.

I wondered why she did not pooh but made water. Usually, like human being water first then stool would follow unless one has diarrhea. Happy made her water & that was it, folks.

When I remembered prior to bringing her outside I picked her pooh on her usual bathroom in the house that explained why she did not pooh outside.

It took me time to figure it out until Joel, my guardian Angel, whom I considered, my memory, reminded me. Joel saved me to buy, Prevagen.

Believe it or not it works. If you don't believe why not try it. It does you no harm. If you do believe, Thanks God, the devil is not with you.

I sat down on my green chair outside with her beside me. Happy, though old is brave. Whenever she would have "regla". Postie in 69 positions would try to make love with her. In public because dog is free from malice and sin. He is God's perfect creature.

But one wink and Potsie would stop his foolishness. He knew what was coming a bite of his "tail" for lack of respect to an old "woman", old enough to be his grandmother. Unbelievable!

Well, after 4 decades of my sorrowful mystery on my green chair I stood up & brought Happy inside the House.

Inside the house Potsie expressed his disappointment by urinating near my favorite breakfast food, my Croissant as his revenge. *Bastos ning ero-a!*

He did not expect me to get upset because he knows I give love what little love he only has himself for me. Amen.

What has this to do with Pandemonium? Good question! Do you know that there is something common among animals just like human beings?

My article COVID-19, which was edited by Tonette published in our local paper, a virus I call "Pandemonium". why?

Because this virus like devils is violent and kills people regardless of if they are good or bad people: harvest time for good elderly people to go to Heaven at the same time harvest time for bad young people to go to Hell. Welcome to the next article: THE PANDEMONIUM, part II.

ON COVID-19

Pope Francis thinks the COVID-19 is a tragic event and not a "Divine punishment." While he might be right, I'm honestly inclined to think that this event is to add and not necessarily to argue a "Chastisement."

(This pandemic reminds me of what Moses instructed his chosen people to keep them safe during the Passover; to lockdown at home and paint the door with the blood of the lamb. So, the Angels of death (CD-19) would pass over their house and spare them).

Chastisement appears to me as one level down to a more serious "Punishment." As we are lockdown in our homes, we become aware of our own strengths and weaknesses. There are two ideas that came in my mind:

First, the awareness that most of the young people, ironically, the lockdown strengthened their own weaknesses of alcohol & marijuana use. This is evident in the sale surge of illicit drugs.

Second, the awareness on the existence of the good seniors, (I think that this virus is more addressed to them). In fact, it appears like a harvest time of seniors, and for them, to whom Christ refers as, "Good people" to go to Heaven.

Jesus, essentially said, "I did not come for good people because they are already saved; I come for sinners to save them from Hell that they might reign with me in Heaven."

The idea that the name of the virus has 19 on it is significant for me because when this virus was surfacing it was around March 19th, the feast of St. Joseph, a silent worker, perhaps joining St. Peter at the gates of Heaven.

The "19" could also mean that this virus has an average of 19 horns. To dispel my innocence, not necessarily my ignorance, please correct me if I am wrong. My email: e_abear@hotmail.com

Therefore, this serious tragic event is a harvest time for good seniors to go to Heaven. I think I would survive this pandemic because at age 82, I fall short to be considered as a "Good senior," with my wife as my witness.

It is also good to remember that St. John Paul II said, there are more Saints going to Heaven in this century more than all the Saints in the past combined. Perhaps, this pandemic brings some truth to St. John Paul II's statement all along.

LESSONS LEARNED FROM
LOCKED IN DUE TO COVID-19

I'm locked in to see & feel if there is God. Humanly speaking, I am only (Matthew 18: 1-5) a little child on the lap of Jesus. Hope he won't mind. I forgot my diaper.

The bad news is that this "new virus" is now surging in Europe. To quote from TV, some scientists think it is "the result of wearing mask & distancing." Like Thomas, I doubt unless it touches America. I hope not. Or not yet.

Indeed, we cannot beat what God has allowed, Satan to release his mutating C-19

(NOTE: "19" is incidentally St Joseph's feast day to remind us to pray to him to change the pathway for this virus with 19 horns to destroy us).

It appears to me that this C-Virus is happening as Spiritual World War III. A bitter taste what World War III would look like as Jesus prophesied (Matthew 24:7).

May this vaccine "deliver us from evil". Amen.

Since C-virus with 19 horns is a killer & murderer, it could not be from God. Common sense, it was created by Satan from Hell. God appears to have allowed Satan. What for? Of course, for chastisement. What else!

There is no question, God is Pro-life while Satan, in human forms, is Pro Choice (to include the choice to murder baby in the womb). Clever is not it? Some people are not that clever that is why they are in for good.

He got me many times over when I was young & careless; no less than when I am old. The more I've sinned, the more opportunities by atonement I get closer to God. Holiness as Christ said, "is a narrow road to Heaven" (Matthew 7:13).

One thing beautiful with God, he did not take away the power, the gifts, and the pride of Satan prior to his fall.

What gifts God give away He appears not to take away. Free Will embodied in conscience is God's best gift to every human being. Gifts, we can love or ignore. Otherwise, what is free will for?

Satan is (as he claimed to be) like "God" except he is the light of darkness (Lucifer) that shines in the darkest night like bats & wolves "who" see better to whom they may devour at night

That is why, Jesus said without the intercession of the Mother of God to our heavenly Father & the Holy Spirit it is impossible for human beings to be saved. "Nobody is perfect" (Matthew 5:48).

There is no credit for us to earn Heaven but no need of credit to fall into Hell. For hell is man's own making.

Some gifted Scientists & other individuals regardless of their vocations or professions in life because due to lack of humility they have already fallen into Hell long before they have died.

That is why, Christ said, "Learn of me for I am meek and humble of heart" (Matthew 11:29). Hence, our humble prayers can save some of their lives. America & some countries are apparently becoming more Hellenistic that we need, I repeat, is chastisement from God to wade out some undesirable people who are, "dressed like sheep's but are wolves' underneath." And good people to go to Heaven (Matthew 9:10: Luke 21:10). What more I can? Tell me.

e_abear@hotmail.com

The fairy tales of:

BLACK LIVES MATTER

God formed a man out of the dust "in his own image and likeness" (Genesis 1:27) and put him in the oven. It so happened that his dog turned loose; so, he went out and found his black dog a mile away eating a dying lamb.

Back home when he opened the oven the man, he created was over cooked & appeared black as the "pit from to pull."

The black man thanked God and said from his heart, "Praise you, my Lord, for many of us would come after me, indeed, Black Lives Matter. In fact, when I opened my eyes, my sclera was white and my teeth were ivory white, at least in the dark of night I could be identified (henceforth, my brothers and sisters would be treated as human beings), worthy of respect, dignity, and honor."

"Sorry Lord, I cannot stand in Heaven among the blonde & blue-eyed Angels unless by "hook or by crook" I get a worldwide attention, I repeat, your message (as I understand it) that "Black Lives Matter."

God said, "Do you remember when I was asked the difference between God and Government?

I tossed a coin, (Matthew 22: 17-22) one side is God (*Hari*) and one side is the Government (*Patay*), held together by my Son's two greatest commandments. The second is, "Love your neighbor as yourself (Mark 12:28-31)." Do no violence but sow love instead for your reward in Heaven is great.

STATUE OF GEN. MACARTHUR

It was on December 7, 1941 (Feast Day of the Immaculate Conception) when Pearl Harbor was attacked by the Japanese's Kamikaze planes that destroyed ships, killed 2,403 U.S. Marines, sailors & 68 workers that America was preparing to defend the Filipino people.

By then, the defenseless *Pinoys* were attacked by the Japanese forces without mercy & easily conquered it hands down.

Not to mention, it was rumored, that Capt. N. Villamor, a West Point Graduate from U.S. knocked out about 27 Japanese planes single handed over the sky of Manila Bay.

Unfortunately, Gen. Douglas MacArthur was cornered under troop strength in Bataan, Philippines. An emergency arrangement was made for Gen. McArthur to escape from the Philippines to America.

His escape from Bataan to Manila harbor was made possible by 250 elite Philippine Scouts who guarded along the route to Manila where a submarine was waiting to bring him out of the Philippines. With him on board were Pres. Manuel Quezon, Gen. Carlos Romulo & some staff members. They arrived in Australia.

Before Gen. MacArthur left Australia in memory of those 250 elite Philippines Scouts led by Capt. J. Villamor who 98% perished fighting against the Japanese soldiers for their successful escape Gen. McArthur promised," I shall return!"

On April 1, 1944, not fool's day but a happy day, the Japanese soldiers like dogs run away with their short tails between their legs out of Philippines.

Along the way of their exit, they performed *"Kempetai"* that is, they killed children, women, old people without mercy. They were the Black Lives Monkeys in Asia, violent & shameless. In Filipino language, *"Walay batasan, mga bastos!"*

On July 4, 1946, there was an unprecedented celebration, a mammoth parade: Filipinos were waving the American flag, singing, "God bless America, land that I love."

A poem in this occasion was composed by Aurora A. Minoza, PhD., a graduate from Fordham University, New York & former President of the University of the Philippines in Cebu City, Philippines.

"I SHALL RETURN"

"When the light of hope is fading for the peace we long have grieved, Fix your thoughts upon the promise loud and clear, "I shall return!""

Don't forget us, have a savior,
led by General Douglas MacArthur who fought & bravely planned, "I shall return!"

Faith and hope will help us get thru which means we shall be free "I shall return"
rings loud and clear, they are at last in our shores!
Rejoice! Thanks God! We shall be free which means will have liberty! Keep it clear
in your hearts, "I shall return!" He has returned!

MY SIX STRINGS GUITAR

PROLOGUE: In Argao I used to climb & went behind the chimney of San Miguel Church, trying to catch bats for lunch. This time I failed. No bats for lunch.

Anyway, beside the church was a tall campanario. I went up the stairs with Puerto my friend, I saw the big bell that when it rang it could be heard in the mountain of Lantoy, home of Mangaw!

This big bell was gone, allegedly sold by a priest; I sang *"Dominos vobiscum, kining pari-a gigutum!"* Which was replaced by a small bell that came apparently from a Priest with a small heart & mind.

I tried to sing my prayer; for it was said the highest form of prayer is to sing. I believe that sometime when I sing from my heart, I cry tears of joy!

MONOLOGUE: The following story was how I healed my 6 diseases, God's gifts to me. let us talk about Eye Bota, son of Nong Doro, in Padada: until now I've not met a man who could play 6 strings guitar & smiled & laughed, worries gone.

How did he become blind? It was said when he was a small kid, he got probably measles. He closed his eyes for weeks on end. When he woke up, his eyes became all white that he could hardly see.

People in Argao during that time would call you w/o malice intended for simply easy identification. So, people would call. Him, "Eye bota" (blind). I won't tell you how I got my name during those times.

It was said he was able to save 200k pesos when he was hired by young fellow for Harana (serenade) at night at nearby girls for years. Nobody dared to rob him because he could see his money.

On meditation of this fact & in metaphor I am a 6 strings guitar myself, having 6 major diseases, the last string God's gift to me was my Patol! (Seizure). Whenever my 6 strings diseases would act painfully, I suffered so much I happily began to play my 6 strings diseases and smiled & laughed within myself & sang, loud & clear that my wife thought I had gone coco!

Mind you when I was a kid I sang, *"Dominos vobiscum ang Pari gigutom!"*. Hence, my pain & suffering were lost in the symphony of my song! Do you understand, how I heal myself?

EPILOGUE: If someday or soon if I'm not smiling on my coffin get an expert deep into the night & make my face happy as I play my 6 strings guitar on a narrow road to the other side perhaps better than Eye Bota.

A MIRACLE AT PARKING LOT

As a background, I worked as a security patrol officer for one of the largest computer technology providers in the world. In an any given time, my workplace could have thousands of cars parked in huge and sprawling parking lots.

We often, discreetly followed terminated employees to get their vehicle information for security reasons. Terminated employees who gave threats and caused trouble were monitored in the parking lot as they leave.

@ 4:00 pm, May 11, 2015, I was driving patrol when my supervisor called me. He showed me a picture of a male employee whose employment would be terminated at 5:00 pm later. My supervisor's order was when he leaves the building to follow him to his car and record the car's plate number.

My employer does this from time to time when they feel the need for more info and trace of a dismissed employee. Getting a car's plate number is a challenge especially when the car is moving. You only have a few seconds to read and memorize the plate. To make matters more difficult, the bosses were monitoring the event and are waiting for the car info. I said to myself, "*I cannot fail.*"

Since there were 3 employee access doors for the office building where to be terminated employee worked, each door aa patrol officer was assigned to watch. When I got to my assigned door, the parking lot leading from the door was vast and there were about an estimated 200 cars in that corner of the lot. I said to myself, if our target person parked here, his car could be one of these 200 cars. The challenge is that I must be able to spot him early while walking so I could follow him to his car. I looked around for a vantage parking spot with an angle to see him coming.

My heart was racing as the 5:00 pm was nearing and I was in a panic to really find a good spotting location. I was moving from one to spot to another. All this time, I was praying for to the Holy Spirit and the angels to help me. A prayer usually said in time crises.

Finally, I parked on a spot where I thought it was the best. In so doing, I blocked a car parked in a stall. I thought I would just move if the car owner would come to move his car. Staying in that I spot I continued to pray, "Please *Holy Spirit let me get that car info; please Holy Spirit and my angels don't let me fail.*"

Then a radio message came from another patrol officer posted in front of the building. He said that the target subject had come out of the on my side of the building and was heading to my parking lot. My heart raced 120 mph. I waited for a few seconds and soon enough my target came into view.

I was stunned to see that he was walking towards me, and I thought if he would pass me, I would have to turn the car around and follow him. Then anything could happen, like me missing his car. He came walking right in front of me, his faced looked solemn and I knew why it was.

Then he came to the right side of my car and opened the car that I blocked. He could not get out of his parking stall unless I moved my car. I realized I was dead on blocking person's car while praying to the Holy Spirit and angels to help me.

No doubt, the Holy spirit and my angels guided me to where I parked after moving around to find the perfect spot. They delivered my target subject right in front of me and I got all the time to record his plate number.

So, I moved my car after noting his car plate. I purposely did not report over the radio my success in getting the info. A radio call came in asking if I was able to accomplish my mission. I said, "I did." I heard a comment in the background "Good". I knew whose voice was that. It was my boss who was monitoring the surveillance.

And I really did not care much. I was not in the business of wanting to be recognized and praised. I just did my job well with the blessing of the Holy Spirit and the angels. And they gave me a miracle.

Looking back at this amazing event, I asked how could I have parked and blocked that one specific car unknowingly that it was what I was looking for? One car to block out of about 200 cars. My prayer was one of being so dependent on the Holy Spirit and the angels. And no doubt they guided me. I felt so blessed.

By SOE

TO GIVE UNTIL IT HURTS

I was at the Pharmacy parking lot on my way to get Abeth's refill of pills. While I was walking towards the door, I was met by an elderly woman driving a motorized chair.

With a pleading voice she said, "Sir, I need you to do me a favor!" I stopped. I thought she would be asking me to move her groceries into her car.

So, I asked, "How can I help you?" She said, "I am driving to Stockton, and I need some gas money."

Without a word, I reached for my wallet in my back pocket: I had one $10 and $2 bills. I remembered these bills were a refund from the Pharmacist weeks ago. So, with a little bit of hesitancy I gave her my money. This lady had just cleaned out my wallet and she said, "God bless you, Sir." I murmured my return blessings.

At that moment, though I feared a professional pan handler might have hit me, I remembered the words of Jesus, "As you do to your neighbor, you do unto to me" (Matthew 25:40).

It reminded me what my Uncle Elmer said to his son, Butch who turned away a beggar because he was weary this beggar might just buy alcohol or Marijuana who said, "What if Butch, if he were Christ who said, "I was hungry & you did not feed me?" (Matthew 25:40).

A similar incident occurred to me years back in a gas station. While I was refueling my car a heavy set African American lady approached me for a few dollars to buy gas.

She pointed to her car parked beside a refueling station. Apparently, her card did not work and now is asking other motorists for money.

In her car were teenagers and some younger ones. It was almost midnight. She told me that she was driving to a place about 30 miles away and does not have enough gas to get there.

I checked my wallet and no money. Empty. Now, I have no recourse but to use my credit card. We walked to her car by the refueling station and used my credit card to put in gas, $20.00 worth. As I was gassing up a motorist wished me, "God bless you!" Perhaps, the lady approached him but did not have any to give her.

A week after that gas giving incident, I again found myself short of funds (my life is a pay check to pay check affair) to pay my obligations and I had nowhere to go. Just then my beloved sister Arhlene in the Philippines messaged me to come home.

Waiting for me was $40,100 (partial pay) from my late grandfather's lot sold as my inheritance. I have written off that inheritance lot as illegal settlers have built their homes in it and claimed it as theirs. I felt amazed how God would return the little favors I gave to others in need.

I learned that there some virtue in giving until it hurts. Because when you give your gravy the main course is still there to enjoy. But if you slice the main course to share to others that is sacrifice cause it hurts somehow. So give until it hurts. St Francis chased after the robber who took his coat and he was offering his robe, too.

"Glory be to God in the highest. Alleluia!"

By SOE

41 YEARS AGO, TODAY

In 1979, my job as a supervisor for a Pharma company required me to travel out of town (Davao) regularly. On October 16, I left pregnant Abeth who was close to her due date. I drove to Butuan early that day. The following day I received a telegram to come home ASAP as Abeth gave birth.

I drove the 7-hour drive and while driving, my wish was to have another baby boy, as I was so in love with my 3-yr. old son, Mao at that time. I drove straight to San Pedro Hospital. When I entered Abeth's room, Abeth greeted me with a smile saying, "It's a girl." We asked the nurse to bring in the baby as I so eager to see her.

The first time I saw Tonette, I let my eyes feast on her tiny figure. She had dark short hair and large slant forehead. She looked like her Grandpa Pete Lavina. She cried so soft like a newborn kitty's faint meow. I think she was barely 6 lbs.

Right there and then, I felt that my love for her was different from my love for my son. I just felt that I had to really take good care of her. Another beautiful child that I will sacrifice my life for. Happy birthday to my darling Tonette.

Parents On Earth, I think what remains to be said, is that Tonette at this time and age is carrying on your legacy of treating and helping patients. Your legacy will live on. Love you to the moon and back,

Parents on Earth!

A FAT WOMAN ON WHEELCHAIR WAS FISHING

Under Ogdensburg's bridge where a river was flowing, along this scenic park I & my dog named, Pogi were jogging, senior style, slower than a macho man walking.

After one round along the river, not far off we saw a fat woman on her wheelchair was fishing. We came nearer and peeped into her can & discovered about 2 small fishes.

I figured it out she must had been fishing for hours & caught only 2 fishes. Anyway, we watched her on a steel chair a few feet away. Pogi shook his head & seemed to disagree.

Ever since Pogi & I were watching her she began catching big fish one after another. I thought we brought luck to her. I looked into her container while she was getting ready to leave, she had caught about 12 fishes.

I told her that Pogi & I had brought luck for her to have caught about 12 fishes. She said, "Yesterday, when I was alone, I caught 57 fishes".

I looked at Pogi and he seemed to say, "I told you so."

THE LOVE STORY OF NELLY & ROLLY

When I got out of the seminary, luckily, I landed a job at the New Maryknoll Mission in Davao. They needed Visayan natives to teach the Visayan dialect to the new arrival Maryknoll priests.

While working there I took some engineering classes at Mindanao Colleges, where I met Nelly. Since I was only taking a few classes it took me 7 years to finish Chemical Engineering. Nelly left for Manila to take the board exam in chemical engineering.

She never came back to Davao. Got an apartment with her parents in Sampaloc, Manila. She got a job detailing for Pascual Lab.

Two years later I followed her up in Manila, took the board exam in Chemical Engineering.

Then we planned of coming to the USA. She was in a better position to apply for a visa to the US. So, to save money she applied with the plan of getting married before she leaves for the US.

Back then if you have a college degree you can apply for an immigrant visa to the US, they called it "third preference." Two years later she got her visa. So, we planned to get married, but her parents opposed!!!!

That was a big problem. Luckily, I was still very close to the Maryknoll priests. One of my former students, very close friend of mine, Father Edward Gerlock helped me out. He was then taking some courses at Asian Social Institute, near Women's College in Ermita, Manila.

We got married at the Chapel at Asian Social Institute without informing any of her and my relatives. It was a secret wedding. After the wedding, Eddie and his classmates at the Institute had prepared a small wedding party at his classmates' apartment.

Some of the Maryknoll priests who were then in Manila, were present. Father St. Leger gave me $20.00, wedding present. That's what we used for our honeymoon in one hotel in Manila.

At midnight she had to go home to her parents' apartment. We meet on weekends. I was then working for an LPG branch company in Olongapo. So, on weekends I go home to my small room apartment in Makati.

Father Gerlock asked me, "So Rolando, what are you going to use for your airfare to the US?" And I said, "That's ok, Father, they have this fly now pay later thing. We'll apply for it."

And he said, "No, don't worry about that. I can ask some Maryknoll priests if they can lend you some." He came up with $1500.00 from 8 priests!!

Nelly left. Father Gerlock helped me with my visa at the US Embassy. Six months later I landed in JFK, where I was met by my lovely wife, Nelly, and we live happily ever after!!!

VERBAL FIGHT

An "N" (Nigger) is a vain word. Since this word cuts more of the physical rather than the Man behind the skin (as it should be) it is not as damaging as the word "J" word. The "J" word (Jesus Christ) touches the Man behind the skin.

This past week I've witnessed on TV (except EWTN) the verbal fight between black and white. It all started "'triviality" from the skin which later became ugly.

Since the fight turned ugly and a celebrity (in spite of his Mea culpa) lost his job I felt "guilty" to regard the situation as trivial.

The BLM does not think it is trivial plus few white people lost in the vanity of their skin.

I say, vanity because when this game is over silly things, they are the same dust from where they came from. I know this thought is grim, but reality teaches us better than we think.

However, I just don't understand the fight. Filipinos in general prefer white skin than the brown they already have.

I remember I had/have a beautiful niece in the whole world in Mambaling who compared her left arm with a visiting black woman's right arm from LA.

I don't know what the black woman was thinking of my niece. I'm not good at presumption. It is unfair "to whom the bell tolls, it tolls for thee," I mean for me.

But what I was almost sure, my niece was just trying to compare w/o malice who had a darker skin. Fortunately, or unfortunately neither none of them, I suppose, was thinking, white as cold as a snowflake from Haven, not from Heaven.

However, it is a matter of preference (if God would undo it) rather than to blame God for being "prejudicial". Please get that right.

The first time I saw a white man in the Philippines I said to myself, how I wished I was born white.

Therefore, we can say without doubt the verbal fight between black & white appears to be due to lack of soul-searching what lays beyond the skin.

Anyway, I thought, the summer sun in the Philippines had made my skin brown, so I stayed indoor. Beside the fact that staying indoor was boring it did not work. I'm brown. Oh, boy!

Maybe, some white people love my brown skin. Not to make me aware to be proud of my brown skin, they have a new name: they called it "tan skin". A much better word than skin "plagiarism."

If you don't agree with me, sorry I don't want to enter into verbal fight, if I could help it, about skin colors which I think is silly & foolish.

I know of a white holy Maryknoll priest who stayed long under the Sun on the beach nearby. He came to me proud of his tan skin. I thought, he was not foolish but wise of the world.

I did not see him for a week. I supposed his tan skin peeled up. Why? Because when I saw him: he looked like an "albino". "Albino" appears like a mixture of white & brown skin. One can save his money from a tattoo-Artist.

Note: Rev. published, Advance News, 4/12/17

TREMENDOUS TRIFLES
FOR CHRISTIANITY

This seems a perfect tremendous trifle for Christianity to fail and Socialism & Marxism to rise if left unchallenged.

For you to digest or reject in terms of today's statistic with regards to clergy's abuse in many layers of human weaknesses, yet it is way down below in statistic during the time of Christ.

The media in general does not mention this statistic as usual because it seems to contradict their hidden agenda of fostering chaos & violence in 37 States in America.

Hence, listen to Fox News, Ch. 56. to get a "fair & balance," news coverage. For your soul-searching peace of mind, try Ch. 35, EWTN and compliment yourself by passing CNN, Ch 17.

This triumvirate like the Three Divine Persons can form one angle of wisdom in our part, a conviction that is strong to stand against what might be our morally decaying culture, America.

One imprudent conclusion today is: if one drop of ink into a gallon of crystal water turns the whole gallon blue, so one abusive clergy turns all the clergies (Nuns as well) bad?

And to add insult to injury to this conclusion they further say, "They are all birds of the same feathers: they flock together." Then, they left their Savior, the Church who is Christ for another savior who else?

Notice that though these tremendous trifles of false conclusions are based on nature which Satan is good at. They forgot that the simile should be based on human term, not in nature.

For example, starting from Christ, if one of His 13 Cardinals was bad (Judas), does this mean that the 12 Cardinals who were martyred, preaching the Word of God the Father are bad? That is, if one member of your own family is a drunkard does it mean all members are drunkards?

To bring this argument from human weaknesses rather than from nature (which God has essentially perfected to serve human being like Cats, dogs & birds) these arguments of one drop of ink or birds of the same feathers are not only imprudent but people who concluded are perhaps unaware that they are all, with all due respect, out of mind.

So, if today one Cardinal is abusive does it mean all about 132 Cardinals including Pope Francis are abusive & bad? Where is the caput? Shall I say, "Dominus Vobiscum?

Again, in the context of Christ's experience, after he performed miracles (First Person as authoritative) many of the Disciples believed Him at first.

But when Jesus said, "I am the Son of God." Some Disciples (forgot the I) scooped, snared, & said "This man, a Carpenter who helped his father, Joseph to do carpentry work in my house for a living said, "He is the Son of God? Wow!"

Most people in Nazareth despite the miracles Jesus did, they drove Him out of town & Jesus escaped to avoid stoning, in his own hometown. And Jesus never returned to Nazareth, *nang lo-od intawon ang atong Gino-o pastilan!*

And disappointed Jesus said to his new ordained 13 Cardinals "Will you also go away?" Jesus was ready to start from the scratch. And Simon Barjona (Peter) said, "To whom shall we go when you have the Word of eternal life!"

Jesus answered to Simon Barjona, "Blessed are you for your flesh & blood (Eucharist that nourishes & sanctify our souls) have not revealed it to you but my Father in Heaven."

I mentioned this last episode to link the rejection of Christ before and during our time esp. in America where Marxism which was rejected in Germany & Russia is emerging in 37 American States.

Black Lives Matter movement, it appears, cannot give love what in their heart of hearts they do not have. But anger, hatred, murders = the Devil's garbage from Hell. Plus joining with the BLM, rioters, looters, and murderers form a tremendous trifle in contrast to the Three Divine Persons something to recon with.

I think, God allowed this "Perfect trifles" (Pandemic, BLM, & rioters and looters) because wealth in America of different colors has neglected the colorless soul that God has endowed in every creature w/o discrimination & leave the vanity of the colors for stupid people to quarrel, past, present & perhaps future.

Oh, how the fallen Angels are laughing: they can hardly count the souls falling into Hell right now. Well, where are we going from our temporary house into a permanent home? Any comment write to me, e.abear@hotmail.com Or hold your peace!

WHERE THE SOCIETY OF ANGEL OF PEACE STANDS

When you think of a place 56 kms. South from Cebu City think of Argao. In Cansuji's hinterland where we once lived in a world we've thrived on *Tingling* and *Camoteng-kahoy*.

Standing on Tanawan's hill, one can see San Miguel Church where from its tower, a huge Spanish bell rang to call its faithful to Mass every morn. It was replaced with a new one.

In Argao, names of heroes who built this town are seen in every street. This is a peaceful place. I'm the 12th seed from a humble family with 14 brothers & a sister who were born here.

In Argao where almost all people are related with one another, I could say with pride - this is a place "Where abortion did not wipe a village."

Today, in Lamakan where once we had a sugar mill, there stands now up on a small hill, St. Miguel Monastery overlooking the whole town between trees.

Within this Monastery, the Sisters of the Society of Angels of Peace live in peace & harmony. It was founded by the generosity & love by Msgr. Chris E. Garcia.

Every morning at the break of dawn one can hear the Franciscan Sisters (SAP) are heard singing for the greater glory of God & peace to all men of good will. Amen.

A NICKEL FOR LENT

My dear people of Ogdensburg I may ask you to do penance for Lent. Regardless of your religious beliefs let us pray for the "disinformation" or good deeds of our Gov. and for the atonement of our sins.

As usual at 6:45 AM I attend Mass in the small chapel of Notre Dame Church. This time I was not in a hurry lest my pajama would be part of my pant. Rarely it did happen.

Mind you if I were two blocks away, I doubt if I would attend Mass everyday with Fr. James Shurtleff. I am not a religious man.

However, living across the Church, my guardian Angel, named Joel would not excuse me. You are lucky if you don't believe in Angels like Padre Pio to whom his classmates in Grade 1 probably thought he was weird.

As usual the Mass was over in 30 minutes. The seniors some much younger than I was were on the way out. Few talks about the events of the day.

Mind you, this was Lent so I decided to stay behind to pray the 14th stations of the Cross. I needed some answers from Heaven with some of my spiritual problems. Do I pray only when I'm in need? You bet I do.

I stood up to do the first station unfortunately I tripped my right foot & bang! I fell with right knee first. The devil did me and not the kneeler. That was the price I thought since I was no longer the friend of the devil I used to be.

My Joel could have been in the washroom. Just guessing. I did not turn around for someone who might have witnessed.

But Mr. Can came & said, "Are you alright?" I answered, "I just fell for the time ahead of Jesus." I wondered if he heard me. Some seniors like me were hard hearing.

At home I raised my pants. I saw my wound the size of a nickel at least better than a penny. I said, "For the nickel; Praise the Lord."

Published, Advance News, 2/29/09.

IN ANOTHER WORLD

What other world has the "mobs" missed other than earths? Last July 4th weekend, when seven black children were shot dead & went to another side of the world, did the lives of these children, ironically, really mattered to them?

Their mobs have toppled down the statues of our "Father figures" with their principles that we believed in. Their motive of "Racial inequality & injustice" appears as an excuse. Perhaps they do not know what a "Father Figure" is, as they might have lacked it in their lives as well as their souls.

Naturally, their souls, empty of love & compassion, are full of anger. Surely, most of them might have come from broken families, who lacked a "Father figure." They have taken out their anger on the statues, what could have been their ideal father thru whose fault is it other than their own foreboding.

They have not reconciled with the past, which they had not encountered. The past that belongs to our tradition & heritage, which we are proud of, for which was fought, won, healed, sealed, & forgiven for by God, and our Heroes as well.

No rational reason should resurrect the past to distract us at the present time where there are so many things more important to be done for America to be great again.

The past is dead & something we can learn rather than try to unlearn & live in the past. The present is all we have to fulfill, our American dream!

Why is it some people born from broken families have had their upbringing taught them fear and love for their Father in Heaven; so, in their lack of "Father Figure" they have God, the Father to take out their frustrations or anger on and heal their wounds, what their earthly fathers would have done have they not left them.

One outstanding person in our present troubled society in America, a product of a broken family is Mother Angelica, whose Father left her Mother when she was only 9-years-old.

In spite of her lack of "Father Figure," Mo. Angelica was spiritually nurtured by her own Mom, taught her fear & love for "our Father who art in Heaven" who dwells in every heart of those who love and adore Him.

For her mom's livelihood she was a laundry woman in Ohio, Mo. Angelica's job at age 9 was to drive an old 4-wheel truck to bring newly washed clothes & picked up dirty clothes for her poor Mom to wash. A humble life for years that God the Father's heart was moved with compassion and love.

As Mo. Angelica grew up, God guided her to be the founder of the Eternal Word Television Network (EWTN). During this time of Civil unrest & Corona Virus pandemic, Catholics all over the world have benefit from EWTN since they can hear Mass every day from Birmingham, AL.

God who is all knowing (in my humble human understanding) might have in mind long before this destructive "mobs" & Corona Virus Pandemic existed.

Hence, God generously created this Network (EWTN) for Mo. Angelica to share globally to all Christians & people in all walks of life the love of God's redemption for all mankind.

Our Government's Constitution probably is the only one in the whole world was entrusted under God by our founding Fathers, whose Faces were carved in Rushmore, South Dakota. If our Constitution is UNDER GOD who could be against God?

THE GATE OF HEAVEN

You don't have to study Catechism to go to Heaven, neither for Muslim's faith to obey in order to ride on a golden chariot to arrive at the gates of Havana. Or perhaps any other religious Faith that teaches people what Heaven is like to get to heaven. Yet, it is written, "No man has seen or heard the happiness prepared for you & I in Heaven" (1 Corinthians 2:9).

God endows every human being the gift of conscience. "Why is it a gift?" Conscience is not owned by every human creature. It's obviously God's gift to man subjecting them to be accountable of it when their life is over.

Therefore, when this temporary life is finished you & I would have to stand on a 90-weighing scale. If it tilts 90 degrees up, you go to Heaven. Which proves you live a saintly life. If it tilts 90 degrees down, you go to Hell. No question or argument.

In case, it is even, it appears the justice of God comes in: you go to Purgatory like dirty clothes to be washed spotless clean. For no one enters the Gate of Heaven who is not a Saint. It is as simple as that. If you don't believe, it's okay. Satan loves you for being like him in Hell.

Conscience tells what is good or bad for us. You know that. So, we can say that God is so great; He gives us, another but greater gift than conscience:

He gives us Free Will, the right to choose between good or evil.

Speaking as a mere human being, God does not take his gift back. Nevertheless, you alone can do it. Gift can be thrown away. You know why?

Doing good, is self-giving with no motive of any return. It is a hard choice. But in the long run it makes us holy and pleasing before God. Why is it hard? Virtuous life is a hard life to live because it involves self-sacrifice. Jesus said, "You've to die to yourself & come to follow me for your reward in Heaven is great" (Matthew 5:12).

It reminds us of the story of a rich a man who came to Christ & asked, "What do I lack in order to enter at The Gate of Heaven?

Jesus answered him, "Leave everything you have, come & follow me for your reward in Heaven is great" (Matthew 19:16-30).

The rich man left & went away sad because he could not leave everything he had. Had he obeyed Christ his name would have been known today like Simon Barjona who left his fishing industry & even his name to whom Jesus changed to Peter, the Rock of the Church.

To emphasize further: Virtuous life is hard to live, when doing bad; the vanity of the world is an easy choice, because it is a vice. Nevertheless, I don't have to tell you the consequences of a bad choice. You know what happened to Cardinal Judas Iscariot.

God is still the refuge of many until now, be you a priest, man or woman of prestige, heterosexual, or homosexual (nothing wrong of being born one of these) as long as one obeys God's two greatest Commandments.

The Gate of Heaven awaits the good man just as the Gate of Hell awaits people of bad choices. I'm not saying, Pro Choice, when ironically there is no choice for someone in the womb. Be it born out of rape or incest.

You find Pro Choice parading in the streets, holding placards, "Abortion should not be banned." I suppose they would have no objection if they were aborted. There is no excuse for murder. Tell me if I'm wrong.

What if it were you in the womb, does common sense makes a difference? People without conscience like the President of America who was confronted about sex differences he said, "Sex does not matter" apparently in the same way as saying, "Life does not matter." It makes no difference, how come?

Just as conscience is alive to those who are in the habit of doing good it is also dead to those who are constantly in the habit of doing bad. Which eventually doing good defines a good man, for example like St. John Paul II, Padre Pio, & many others in Heaven.

Now, what can we say about a good man? "A good man, "Christ said, "Does not need salvation." Why? They are already saved. That is why, Christ said, "I've come to save sinners." For what? Believe it or not - to reign with him in Heaven forever.

Do we owe Christ who died on the cross to save sinners like some of us a favor? No. He is God & owes no favor from us. Why? He is the Triune of God, the author of life, and everything that exists. A mystery of love no man can fathom just as a dog cannot fathom human wisdom, why they don't walk like him naked?

On top of this, God who is so good, He offers mercy through St. Faustina for us in order to obtain peace of mind & soul. The recalcitrance or to say the least among us, the stupid who made bad choices: you know less of me, do you?

Therefore, just as the gate of Hell awaits the bad people & so are good people & the repentant sinners await at the Gate of Heaven.

Rossana's diary on:

ROSSANA'S DIALOGUE

11/21/1997

This morning on my way to work, I got a chance to contemplate on a lot of things, for instance, I watched people walk by on the road and people waiting on the bus.

One particular thing that caught my attention for some reason was a woman enjoying her cigarette. It so happened that I gleaned on my right while waiting for the light to change.

I watched this woman on my side mirror, and I heard myself talking without thinking "Help her Lord to quit smoking."

For a moment I was very quiet and wondered to myself where my thoughts came from. I asked myself if it was any of my business to meddle, my thoughts continued to run off asking God how I could make this world a better place to live.

I left my thoughts wondering as I went to work. Puzzled as I was, I still managed to concentrate on my work.

On my way home that same day, I drove in silence and had forgotten what transpired earlier this morning.

My mind was at peace that nothing could bother me in any way. All of a sudden, I had an urge to listen intently that I could not ask for anything more but silence.

I felt that someone took my hand and placed it close to my heart so I could listen attentively.

I heard Mama Mary's voice so loud in my mind as she gave me the message that I could help a person change for the better by fasting and constant praying. It felt like I was in a trance while driving and somebody just snapped their fingers in front of me to get me back to reality.

I sat in amazement of what happened. I caught myself smiling without even knowing and I heard myself saying "Ma, thank You for answering my prayer and be with me always."

INTENTION:

"Through Mary to Jesus", Lord may we always keep this in mind that through Mother Mary prayers are answered and favors are granted.

THE GREY NUNS

In the early 19th century, Ogdensburg was brimming with vibrant, young, and energetic Grey Nuns. To serve the people's body and soul they founded the Hepburn General Hospital.

Gracefully, they have left the community. I wanted to write or email them. But someone said (in T.S Eliot's paradigm of the Antwerp), "They went home to another country and have left no addresses."

Anyway, mysterious as it might have been, I found their addresses in the Chapel of Notre Dame. I write in prayers. They answer by deeds whenever I miss a step and get hold of the rail, or nearly side-swept by a passing car because of my tunnel vision, or simply a smile from my "enemies."

There are few of them now. With perhaps their aching knees and hard backs, unyielding to the pleasures of staying late in bed, I see them at 6:30 AM, in the Chapel of Notre Dame. They worship a Live Jesus, all wrapped up substantially present in the glory and mystery of Jerusalem, a dead Word for "bread."

Every time I see the Grey Nuns, it reminds me of what happened in the '70s when the seed that Mary Sanger planted in 1915 found it's celebration when the Supreme Court allowed the killing of babies in the womb, an issue and reverberates until now among the good, the bad and the ugly Americans.

The houses of the senate and congress seem to have more Mary Sanger' mentors in the perpetuation of this silent "holocaust." A reflection of our moral values,' melting down against the increasing deceptive concept of relativism where truth is subject to the individual's interpretation and not by God's appointed Magisterium.

Every time I see the Grey Nuns, it reminds me of what happened in the '70s when coincidentally quite a number of nun and priests left their vocations, after 15 years of being a professed nun.

What was worse than a bad decision she divorced Christ and remarried an ex alcoholic unemployed priest and lived in poverty perhaps preferable to comfort of the convent and its prestige that God in His divine providence has so provided to those who are faithful to him.

Awarded by Pope Paul VI as one of the TEN MOST OUTSTANDING FAMILIES from the entire Philippines, the scandal of our family must have shaken perhaps the Heaven badly that my father, four brothers died one year after another. Heaven spoke and it was not good. We mourned for the death of what seemed God's glory in us.

Other brothers of mine seeking holiness elsewhere are dancing with the Masons. This is not to say in understatement that there is something "unholy" with the masons, but they may have "holiness" that a simple uninformed Catholics like me could only envy. But I would stand by Peter, come high and low water.

Like Christ's naked exposure on the 10th Station of the Cross, I seem to find my gradual healing by exposing our family's own nakedness by writing, ironically a shameful legacy that might strengthen the weak, discouraging the weaklings. Or hopefully emboldened the strong.

Every time I look at the few Grey Nuns almost every 6:30 AM in the chapel where God is alive and well, I am reminded that they could be equal to a hundred good people in Ogdensburg.

If Sodom and Gomorrah had a hundred good people surely God would not have roasted them in what Christ honestly said, into the "everlasting fire where there is gnashing and grinding of teeth."

A worried senior complained to Fr. Pavone, "What about seniors who have no teeth to grind?" And smiling from his "pulpit" Fr. Pavone said, "Don't worry, teeth (cheap dentures) will be provided."

HOW CAN I COMPLAIN?

In 1978, my wife & I were in Canada. We settled in Vancouver, B.C. While she was taking her first year Residency in Pediatric at the Vancouver General Hospital, I applied for a Residency in Internal Medicine.

Since I had two years of Residency in Internal Medicine at Bohol General Hospital, Philippines, I was confident I might be accepted. Unfortunately, I was rejected.

The reason was that they only accept foreign students who obtained 80% in the ECFMG exam. After saying a long prayer to God before the exam, I held the rope of 75% before I would have fallen into Hell of academic failure. How can I complain?

Imelda's grade was 80%. It was no surprise to me because the Dean in our school at C.I.M. had recommended her as one of the first top ten students in class of about 40 students.

Anyway, the V.G.H. had allowed me to tag along with 4 Residents doing their first-year residencies in Psychiatry. Some were foreign students.

From their sympathetic eyes they were perhaps told that I had the privilege to be with them. How can I complain?

Since the pressure on both of my eyes seemed painful after reading, I pressed my eyeball to relieve it. I felt better.

I consulted an eye specialist at the Vancouver Hospital for perhaps a new pair of eyeglasses. The Doctor discovered that in fact I was suffering from chronic Glaucoma for the past several years.

After he prescribed me an eye drop, he told me that even with my eye drop to control the pressure I would be completely blind after 20 years. I believed him. How can I complain?

Anyway, that was 42 years ago. I can still see. I went to the eye specialist at Claxon Hepburn Hospital in Ogdensburg, New York. I asked her for how long I would be able to see before I would get completely blind.

She prescribed me, Torzolamide, 1 drop 2x a day. She said that I would be able to see with my tunnel vision thru the rest of my life. I believed her. How can I complain?

Footnote: with my tunnel vision I could focus from my shrunken forgetful brain at age 83, to write more accurately my prose & poetry.

What more I could see what I took for granted for several years the beautiful eyes of my wife, sparkling like the Angel above. Thanks to Dr. Nguyen. I felt comfortable. How can I complain?

THE 2ND JUDGEMENT

"Lock your door" as God, the Father, said "and pray." That is why I've always a small room in my house where I can pray, a legacy I've inherited from my father, Juan.

Hence, have a Bible in your house which contains the Word of God. Let us meditate particularly about the 2nd coming of Jesus" (Matthew 24: 29-30), which involves our 2nd judgement. How will this affect our lives?

We know not, when will be the end of this world for even the Angels in Heaven or Satan do not know. Christ said: "Be watchful." Let me start my discussion with you:

When our Lady "died" at age 70 she appeared in Fatima as a 16 yrs. old Lady. Unlike us, she was conceived without original sin, the 2nd Eve. Ven. Bishop Fulton J. Sheen often referred to.

Our new Eve who did not understandably have to wait at the end of the world to recover her body unlike us who pray daily believing, "the resurrection of our body & life everlasting" (Credo).

So, when we die (as all of us do) our souls would be 16 yrs. old and we have to wait at the end of time to recover our 16 yrs. old bodies from the dust that once our Heavenly Father crested, not made.

By that time, we will be as wise as the Angels in Heaven. We can read each other's mind without talking. A gift we recover when our first parents lost when they disobeyed by eating the forbidden fruit in paradise.

We will be judged for the 2nd time by God. Can you imagine souls from Heaven, Purgatory & Hell will face judgement of the "dead" and the "living" bodies before God?

We look forward again for this event to take place as we pray further, "I believe in the resurrection of the body & life everlasting. Amen."

In our prayer we understand the word, "dead" to mean are souls from Hell who were faithful to Satan and the word "living" are souls who were faithful to God.

At the end of your short life in this world will you be among the "Living" or the "dead" standing before the throne of God? It would entirely depend the kind of life you lived while you were on earth.

The Angels in Heaven & all the Devils in Hell will all come out to be judged for the 2ⁿᵈ time too. Remember, what the Devil said in Gerasene when he saw Jesus:

"Son of God, are you coming to torment us before our time?" Which means their torment would be increased terribly at end of time (Mark 7:8-29).

Anyway, how beautiful it is to be in Heaven which Christ referred that "no eyes have seen, nor ears have heard the place I have prepared for you."

Don Bosco, having seen colors never seen on earth thought he saw Heaven. And the Angel said, "What you see is only the basement of Heaven."

If this world is so beautiful, colorful Robins chirping in trees, the scent of cherry blossom, ducks from Brazil eating the young grass during springtime are so beautiful things to see. If this is beautiful what must be the beauty of Heaven like?

How terrible it is to fall into Hell with our body to suffer being burnt and would never be consumed forever when we cannot even stand a minute with our finger over a burning candle. How much more with our bodies!

God, the Father knew this place created by Satan, but God has allowed because He does not get back the gift (as gift should be) of free will & conscience to all His creatures: the choice between good & evil, between "Pro-life" or "Pro-choice."

So, God, our Father, does not want us to fall into Hell that He sacrifices "his only begotten Son" to forgive our sins and save us from the fire of Hell into Heaven.

My father who read the Bible from cover to cover used to tell me: "How lucky & happy are those who witness the end of time" (Luke 21:11): famine, earthquakes, fire, flood that until now I don't understand.

At last, at the end of time there will be no more Purgatory only Heaven & Hell. The faithful of God will enter the golden gate of Heaven while lost souls will fall into the furnace of the fire in Hell.

To a man who told Padre Pio, "I don't believe in Hell." Padre Pio with a smile on his face said, "You will believe it when you will be there."

Caution: watch for the devil far wiser than us how he would twist the truth with tantalizing words that when we experience the pleasure of sin is a lifetime of regret that we have offended the Lord.

The hope is the more we sin ironically with our atonement we get closer to God like that womanizer St. Augustine thru the prayer of St. Monica, his mother, was converted & became the Bishop of Hippo.

Pray for those who know what they are doing is wrong because they are not covered what Jesus said from the cross, "Father forgive them, for they do not know what they are doing."

FOR YOUR INFORMATION

This new virus now spreading in 7 States except in New York, some scientists believe is more deadly than Covid-19.

It appeared to have originated in France. Now, let us blame France as we did with China for Covid-19. If either by our confused mind, to whom or to which place shall we blame?

NEWS: Our present vaccine is less effective against this new virus. U.S. death at present is 417,000 (1/24/21).

That makes the processing busy at the gate which one should go to Heaven, Purgatory or Hell. That is if you believe those places exist. If you do not believe, shall I say that you believe in nothing?

A good friend of ours, Fr. Jimenez recently passed away from Covid-19. He got it in the Parish somewhere in Watertown where he was serving.

He had retired but he was requested to serve this Parish without a priest. Is he not a silent hero for Ad Majorem Dei Gloriam? This was where he got the Covid-19 virus. He got only one brother, a Surgeon in Florida. Fr. Jimenez finally retired in heaven; I pray.

At present, we cannot go to Canada where we had bought 2 yrs. ago a house in Mississauga in preparation for our retirement this year, 2021.

Our son, Dave is staying there hopefully to lessen the dust, I suppose, his footsteps would help but not in his room, oh ya yay!

If our vaccine won't help because of this new mutated virus from Covid-19 we are not sure if we can go home to Cebu for our 50th Golden Wedding. Pray that we can go home.

From the DNA of my 12 brothers our survival rate is between 70-79 yrs. old. Nobody reached 80. I'm now 84 *pohon*. No one of us reached 90 so 90-84, I'm looking at 4 more years to live, oh ya yay! What door do you think I would enter, knowing my sinful character, H? or luckily P?

My wife is thinking, I should live forever on earth. Am I second to Elijah in the Old Testament who rode on a golden chariot going to Heaven?

Not to mention our mother Mary who assumed into Heaven in August 15 while Jesus "descended into Hell & on the 3rd day he rose again and went into Heaven" and apparently reported to our Father in Heaven, "Mission is accomplished."

By the way, do you know what Jesus said to tormented souls in Hell for 3 days? I have not read or heard a Sunday's sermon from the pulpit?

The mystery is Mama Mary would visit us to mention a few in various places, for examples in Portugal, Fatima, France, Lourdes, and Philippines, Simala, Cebu.

By the way, sometimes I would have thoughts of going to Heaven or cross the red line to Hell. That is why perhaps my wife wants me to live forever on earth.

The devil assigned to me, whenever I think like that, I sense would be laughing, heh, heh & saying, "Elmer, my friend, *wala ba ka makoyape!*"

MY EYE DROP

A little miracle happened today. Yesterday, I knew 2 places where I usually put my eye drops, but I could not find it after looking for it for almost 2 hours.

I went to the extent of running my fingers around my lazy boy, raised my pillow up, *yagyag* (shaken up), raised my blanket high *dugay nang wala malabhan* (unwashed). Just in case it was there, but nothing fell. It only flew my *abog* away, oh boy!

I went all cover the house to search for it. I went to the bedroom and to unfamiliar places or corners that it could have oddly been placed. I pleaded to my angel, Joel, but nothing happened. Perhaps, she is selectively deaf like me. *Pa bongol bongol* like Bebot. I needed a drop before sleeping.

I had a new one unopened, but I could not open it, obeying Imelda that I should finish the one I am using before opening another new one. I used to cheat before but now no more of that "shenanigans." So, I went to bed without it. Poor me.

This noon after reciting 13 rosaries on my knees, I sat down on my lazy boy, and I saw my eye drop bottle on top of my pillow that I *yag yag* (shaken) yesterday.

I asked myself how could that happened? My guardian angel is a worse joker like me. This is not the first time he did it to me. Perhaps, he found my life too boring!

I accepted it as a clear miracle complement by my guardian angel, Joel. Immediately as the devil does that, I should think of a rationale to erase this miracle. I could not help but laugh at my invisible enemy & said "Better next time, Devil, but not this one heh, heh!"

Footnote: These 3 hours of prayer on my knees, I wept 3 times with mix feelings of loneliness & joy witnessing my Calvary soon. Soon, I would arrive, not by my will like Christ's in his agony in the garden but God's, the Father's will be done, (Mark 14: 32-42) not withstanding that if it were in accordance with my wife's will, it would be for me to live forever, and I would have to agree with her. Alleluia!

OUR GOLDEN WEDDING ANNIVERSARY

My niece, Babette showed me 7 pictures of how they spent their 8 years Wedding Anniversary that included spending their precious time out of bed & out of sight, skating on ice. While here in New York, I saw this morning minion delight, a flock of Ducks.

They came from Brazil after weeks on flight, landing on our lawn, eating green grass for the early Springtime. They think in paraphrase like Dr. Jose Rizal that "Early bird & early flight is the step way to eat to be healthy & wise."

Where is my friend, our Ground Hog, or the golden tails of male squirrels (unlike us) to attract the fair looking female squirrels? My pet dog, named Potsie, they are his best enemies. No one passes me without his approval, "bow wow wow!"

When a dog loves he can be jealous like some of us to whom he is faithful & true. The devil beside me thinks that I don't know much about myself.

If you don't believe in Angel read the story of Padre Pio. He played with his Angel before going to school, Grade I. When he told his friend how he played with his Angels they looked at him weird.

You know, very often I'm caught between right & wrong. Psychopath without conscience knows what is right, is wrong & what is wrong, is right. That is why, they seem not to suffer the consequences of sins. Who is better before God, me or the psychopath?

Roy & Babett, I see you both skating, young & beautiful, on ice as far as my glaucomatous eyes can see white snow which covers black & white, brown, or yellow weeds. I think, white flurries of snow are like graces from Heaven which do not have weeds, racial discrimination.

Some people do not seem to understand that underneath the skin we are all the same before God. Where does the word, Racism come from?

Too often, the Rooster that cock is the Rooster that lays his egg. *"Egg itlog man, run dalagan T ang katapusan, Ignorante!"* Not you, but like me when I was young.

It reminded me our stairway to Heaven or God forbid, down to Hell. You know: the 1st time I met my wife, we were sweethearts with faces shining like red apples (unpicked by Robin's at early stage of life) for us to kiss with each other's to satisfy our insatiable thirst for love as you were, no doubt, as sweethearts like us. Am I right?

Then, we got married as lovers do as you are now and then the unhurried passing of time, we get old: no longer sweethearts & lovers we are now but not dried Partners of life like the golden leaves of Maple trees prior Winter's fall. Or dead leaves if you might think so. So, sad as many people think but it is a fact of life we cannot disagree. How is that?

I walk with my 3 feet, with my wife beside me, holding my right arm that I might not fall on the left side into the wrong crowd & GOD forbid I might be lost forever, yellowish amber, is it not? I mean is it hot? What do you think?

You know, hormone like my wife's is younger even with 2 even age-old people who are married like most people do. Scientists sent to space, a male & female monkey. The male monkey died first long after the female did.

It proves why a woman survives longer than man. Why? A woman has high hormone than man in order to survive to deliver a child at birth.

That is why, generally a husband would die first for the wife to bury & weep for the passing of a good partner of life. Man as donor does not give birth to a child, a disordered dream it appears to all transgenders.

I don't know but it must be Heaven sent for me to marry a beautiful woman, 8 yrs. younger than I am. People think with my white hair that I'm walking with my daughter with beautiful black hair when in fact she is my Angel, my wife who knows me better than I do to myself.

You know, old age is a gift from God where some people think like us from earth's Haven, a grasp so far & yet so near to Heaven where time without numbers is a misnomer into a place where God reigns forever with His Angels & Saints, singing a melody we have not heard on earth's show or night clubs.

My handsome, good-looking Brother Mithras was like that. He sang for free with his guitar in night clubs while his wife would patiently wait inside their car sometime till the break of dawn.

How could it be better? The sweet baritone song of Perry Como or the sweet melodious dosing of Pat Boone, hip-hop & twisted melody-feet of Michael Jackson, the improved version of Elvis Presley. They died young at 50 to give us what Heaven is like. For them, it appears the unnecessity of old age. But now, I repeat, as sweet as my Partner in life I have something for you to look forward to; if I survive, to have a simple celebration of our Golden Anniversary on June 27, 2021, with our family circle & the SAP sisters, brothers, & Fathers in the silence perhaps at St. Michael's Monastery in Argao, Cebu, Philippines, God willing 😊. You are invited. Your best gift is your presence. Alleluia! 🏠

MY ELDERLY PATIENTS

(COVID-19 Vulnerable)

Due to my old age, 84, coming this year 2021, I'm most concerned like everybody else about the natural deterioration of all my organs: a smaller brain, a fibrillating heart, a scarred lungs, liver, & kidneys at best at present. I urge you: if you care about your body: have your organs checked. It might surprise you.

What I learnt from my Geriatric clinical experience in 1984, doses of drugs in geriatric patients should be computed according to their weight like pediatric patients.

Unfortunately, a lot of family doctors & even some Specialists who only have a glimpse of Geriatric studies, sorry to say, have unforgivable ignorance of this fact.

When I was doing my Geriatric practice at a Geriatric Center in Newfoundland, Canada, most patients came in confusion with one bag of medicines. Most different kinds of anti-depressant drugs. I suspected that most of them probably did not know where they were going after this life. Look who is talking?

The first thing I did when Geriatric patients came in for admission was to generally discontinue all drugs except for their heart pills or other pills that held the life of other vital organs. The first reaction of these patient was anger & frustration. Why? It is because they have been in the habit of these drugs.

It usually took time for them to discover the correct orientation of their minds. Old people, no exception for me, just like babies but with old, wrinkled faces & often edematous feet. So, most of them walked like old ducks. Not to mention that without their dentures they were no different than milking babies.

The first history taking I did was to assess the orientation of their minds. When I asked each one of them: "What day is today?" Often, I got the answer, "It's Sunday, Dr." instead of Monday. They were often 1 or 2 days in advance. ☺

WHAT HAPPENED TO ME?

What happened to me at age 84? Recently when I told my wife that "Today is Wednesday." And she quickly answered, "You're wrong! Today is Friday." Oh boy, I asked myself, "Why am I, 2 days ahead?"

Was I looking instinctively to go to the other side, perhaps in the anticipation of where I should be at the end of my life, up into Heaven? Down to Purgatory? Or cast into Hell, of everlasting fire of torment & indescribable pain?

On further meditation, let me share with you my little Apologetics about what I learnt from the Jesuits in San Jose Seminary in Manila, Philippines way back in 1978.

It is said, God only knows each & every one of us, even before we were born of our fate. GOD have mercy! Whether we like it or not, life hereafter is what we make it.

We cannot choose because after death we have no more FREE WILL. Our free will after death is dead & taken over by either God or Lucifer. It would depend on how we live our life on earth.

Christ said, if you're a good man you go to Heaven, but if you are a bad man you go to hell. However, if you are neither a good man nor a bad man, you will undergo a Purgatorial life, to be clean enough to enter the gate of Heaven, that is if St. Peter would let you in.

It reminded me when Lucia, Francisco, & Jacinta were asking our Lady in Fatima about where their friend, Amelia was, who apparently committed a mild sin. Our Lady answered, "She is in Purgatory."

And when they asked her how long she would stay in Purgatory before she would go to Heaven, our Mother in Heaven answered, "She will be in Purgatory until the end of the world."

My father seemed right when he said to me, "How happy if you witness the end of the world." Is it a short cut to Heaven? I asked myself, "Better be, no more screaming," said St. Peter.

I had written this joke of Ven. John. Fulton Sheen when he said (not the exact word) that one day our Lord went around to tour some corners in Heaven, and he found some souls who should not be in Heaven.

He went to see St. Peter at the door, prepared some scolding as to why he allowed these unworthy souls to enter Heaven. And St. Peter answered, "Lord, every time I closed the door, your mother opened a window."

Anyway, for Amelia with a mild sin to stay in Purgatory till the end of time, that shocked me, beyond my imagination. If by the grace of God thru the intercession of Mama Mary & the Saints, I would be lucky to end in Purgatory.

For sure, Heaven is not far away where I would be. Thanks God, I'm an old man, given a chance on earth to reflect where I want to go. Do you remember what Christ said in (Matthew 4: 16-17)?

"And for those who sat in darkness have seen a great light and for those who sat in the region and the shadow of death, light has dawned." And from that time Jesus began to preach, saying, Repent, for the kingdom of Heaven is at hand (on earth)."

The above saying, Jesus is consistent when He teaches us how to pray, the "Our Father who art in Heaven...... thy kingdom come thy will be done on earth as it is in Heaven." (Luke 11: 1-4; Matthew 6: 9-10). That means, when we do the will of God on earth, we become the "The image and likeness of God" (Genesis 1:26).

WHEN A DOG FIGHTS A DOG AT THE MIRROR

The "FIVE" program by Mr. Greg infrequently shows about "funny" animals between its program. Honestly, this is why I watch this show other than Fox "Breaking News."

Without these funny animals I don't think I will watch this show. It does not mean that the Five program people do not have good issues to discuss. They have, but the funny animals in this show just attract me, why?

Don't blame me: I'm a dog lover; the name of my dog is Potsie. He sleeps with me in bedtime and snores ahead of me.

If somebody is knocking at the door, I've to do the barking myself, "bow wow wow" before he does. Sometimes, he just let me do the job. He must have thought I'm a dog. It's ok, I'm.

Anyway, let us go back to the Five program. This time (2/3/21) they show a black dog, it appears to me as a Poodle. They showed him a mirror & the Poodle fights back as if he sees another dog at the mirror. The Poodle does not know he is fiercely fighting his own self. Everybody in the show have a big smile while I laugh.

You know for sure: dog does not have the intelligence of a human being. Yet don't rush to judge a dog's failure to recognize himself. Just because he does not understand that he is unknowingly fighting himself. That's the funny thing, I love to see & laugh.

On the higher level of thinking, humbly, I think some people are like this Poodle. How? They fight & impose the light of their own values to some people who are in the dark of their viciousness. It happens whenever they try to impose their own values on others instead of seeing emphatically "as they are."

In other words, we should have to accept people & love them as they are. And instead, silently pray what we want them to be like us. Otherwise, we are like that Poodle fighting unknowingly his own self at the mirror.

Not to mention, what difference does a Poodle's intelligence to some people who impose their own values to some vicious people? Do I get that right? I hope so.

Of course, there is an exception for this, when some bad people impressed of your character ask for your advice. Or a group of people like you and me, attending a Sunday Mass as part of our obligation. If you don't attend the Sunday Mass, you commit mortal sin. Who wants to go to Hell if one suddenly dies unexpectedly?

I remember when I was a kid Brod. Ernesto brought a well-cooked meat. While I ate, I felt hot. I told him, "What kind of meat is this?" He said, "It's a dog meat." Maybe, that is the reason why, I love my dog, Poodle." Anyway, one Sunday I attended a Sunday Mass. We listened to a new Priest for his long sermon, now & then, pausing to check his notes while I was thinking of my Poodle infrequently checking my wristwatch.

Thank God, he concluded his sermon after more than half an hour, that we should be what Christ said, to "Love God above all things and to love our neighbors like the way we love ourselves." The Mass began as we stood up and sang, Alleluia!

MY CANTICLE OF BROKEN RACISM

I pray, "Your love to me my heavenly Father is as simple as the early morning sunrise from the East. It brightens my whole uncomplicated day before my final sunset in the West."

As a mere simple & naive child, I say, "My heavenly Father, your love is a kind of 'color' among people of different races with colors disagreeable to some White, Black, & Asian, not to mention the Red Indians that some of us have left behind in our so called, "Civilization."

Now, residing in upstate New York, I recall when I was 9 yrs. old, during the World War II, a white Marines was in our house. He was a tall man, named Henry, he was there to fix the electricity in our 7-bedroom home in Argao, Philippines.

Our former home, now, if you happened to pass by it on your way to San Miguel Church, you'll see nothing but a pile of rotten woods in disarray. This was the place where once almost all of us, 15 kids were born out of love. Indeed, 13 of my brothers' borrowed lives had returned for good, I hope, to our heavenly Father, Creator of Heaven & earth.

Anyway, the U.S. Marines would like to pass the night after drinking *'bahal'* (40% alcohol) derived from coconut juice we call *"Tuba"* offered by my brothers so they could sleep the night peacefully.

After all, there were no more cruel Japs who occupied the Philippines for 3 yrs. to shoot at: they were like dogs with tails between their legs running out of town ever since Gen. Douglas MacArthur landed in Leyte in 1944.

By the window, I saw for the 1st time a black man, alighted from his truck full of black carbon from upper Kansuji on his way into a convenient store across our home. It was a unique sight to see a black man. He was beautiful among Asians who are browned skin.

I wished as a child (No malice intended to Asians or Caucasians) to trade my skin with black so I would be the only child, proud, unique & beautifully, pure black among my peers in school.

Just in case my heavenly Father would not hear my prayer I stayed longer under the heat of the sun. Well, it never happened. I became a Molato instead. God's will be done as usual. In this life we are not in command unless we think like Soros or less than him, who else but Big Tech or Lucifer. Not to mention some of the so called, Squad.

As a legal Migrant in the U.S. seeking a better life for myself, I was shocked to see the quarrel between Black & White Americans. It never entered into my mind nor understand the racial discrimination of injustice between black & white Americans.

Surely, their might have been some truth in it. My heart is full of love: there is simply no room for misunderstanding or injustice after what I heard from Jesus who said, "Walk on the narrow road...that will lead you to eternal happy life" (Matthew 7:13-14). Hence, die to yourself no matter what enticing vanities there are in this world before your eyes. Hold on to your values.

Jesus is full of love on the cross & so am I trying to be there is no place for anger or back talk or resentment in my heart: there is no I, me, & myself try "it," my Brothers & Sisters in Christ.

The word RACISM was born BROKEN on my mind because it has apparently no dignity & character for those who are preoccupied with it. Perhaps, they have just missed the chastisement allowed by God, mistaken as Pandemic. This word, PANDEMIC does not go beyond the skin of reason.

Beyond the skin of reason is where our faith resides in our respective souls which is the reflection of God's own "image and likeness" (Genesis 1:26) before Eve ate the apple & tasted good and handed the remaining to Adam did their "image & likeness" was lost when simultaneously both of their eyes were opened (Genesis 3:6-7). Their disobedience affects us all till the end of time.

Yet, by His divine Mercy revealed to St. Faustina in 1937 thru Christ from the Father we can earn Heaven by carrying our crosses as Jesus does on the Cross in order to unite all of us as Brothers & Sisters at the end of this world when he would come again & fulfill his promised, "I will judge the living and the dead" (Credo). Alleluia!

THE STORY OF PASTOR

As a Filipino: *I believe this record would explain how proud he was to be a citizen of the Philippines serving in the military. (Too bad I couldn't find his picture with the late President Magsaysay pinning him a medal of courage & distinction).*

As a father: *As for my own personal knowledge about my papa, all I could say is that he is a very responsible father & is a strict disciplinarian to his children and taught us the moral values of life.*

As a husband: *A loving husband to my mama.*

As a brother: *He was a very hospitable & accommodating brother to his relatives who came from the province & would stay with us in Project 4 - no matter how small our house was, he always had a room for them.*

I remember, he would call me (from U.S) telling me to remit some monetary help from his P.I. pension for his brothers (Tio Tonying & Pacio).

Also, he was very thoughtful to his older sister, the late Tia Eva who used to live in Teacher's Village that time. He was in U.S. & would remind me to visit her every once in a while, which I did.

*These are all the kind gestures I remember about my dad. Miss him so much... –**Josie***

By Josephina Sevilla

Self-discordant...

OUT OF MIND & OUT OF SIGHT

I was in my mini chapel praying the 13th Rosary before Mama Mary of Fatima, a beautiful statue beyond compare. It was given to me by my niece, Aida, when suddenly Imelda appeared & gently touched my right shoulder: I felt shaky to get back to reality from my divine environment.

She was in her usual brown coat & pant from the Hospital. She mumbled a few words. I could not understand because I was not wearing my hearing aid: Thursday 6:14 PM, 8/11/21. It was perhaps a reminder that I should walk our dog, named Potsie.

I stood up & looked for Potsie, tied him with his leash, his tail wagging left & right, happy to be outside. Outside, the weather was good. I could see a landscape of green grass that looked like a carpet that was newly mowed lawn. Gone were the stubborn weed of Dandelions, waving her smelly yellow flowers.

When I glanced at the right, I was surprised that Imelda's new Mercedes white car was not parked. I thought a taxi might have dropped her home. I wondered what happened to her car. Accident? Oh no. I prayed to St. Michael daily for her protection.

To be sure, Potsie & I turned back & climbed our four steps hospital staff house. Checked all rooms, bathroom & down 12 steps into the basement where my good wife prohibited me lest I might fall & break my head. At my age, I have a terrible history of falling on my back. Recently, I had a linear fracture of my vertebra; consequently, I passed blood in my bowel. It went away by the prayer.

Anyway, by "conspiracy," Boyet put green tape for every step in case I want to go down into the basement whenever Imelda is not around.

Well, here in the basement: no sign of Imelda hiding, "Hide & seek" for fun whenever I remember the good old days.

I got nervous. Anxiety began to alarm my whole being upside down from inside my brain. Nostalgic, I said, "Lord, where is my only beautiful Imelda?"

Anxiously, I was worried & deeply concerned. (It had never happened before). I hoped and prayed she would show up soon. I imagined worse might have happened.

It was beyond words to write the tragic scenarios played out by the devil so that I would be out of my mind. Indeed, I thought, I was getting out of my mind, but not necessarily out of hope. Or out of sight.

Remember, to refresh your mind, she touched my right shoulder & I felt shaky with my energy getting out of myself so my body could return - calm, compose, and stable at her presence?

What I did, I walked with Potsie, hand down, hungry & nervous. I missed my Croissant snack. So, I went to the Hospital (where she works) to find out, a 45-minute duckling walk, my body wavering between right & left. I was strong enough I left my cane.

Potsie seemed irritated, pulled me harder. I had a hard time catching him up. I said, not in English lest he might understand but, in my dialect, "*nag salig lang ning bo angakay batan on pa ikaw.*" 🐕

Well, this was my first time to come to the Hospital ground. All I wanted was to see her car. There are several buildings. I did not know what building the Hospital was. The buildings looked alike to me.

After checking the cars on their respective parking lots, I could not find Imelda's car. No people were loitering around for me to ask. I tried to knock on doors that indicated "push." I pushed, and no doors were opened. Oh, yay, yay! 🐌. What happened to me!

I was down to the last building where two police cars were parked. I was lucky, and I saw a young lady out of her car hastily going into the building. I could not catch up with her. ☺

Remember, I walked with measured steps like an old Duck. So, when I reached the gate & opened the door: it was locked. So, I did not know which doors she entered.

I knew I was in the hospital because at the entrance was the parking signed, "Dr. on call." But there was no car parked in front of the sign. So, Imelda was not on call. Anyway, I got hold of one door. I pulled the handle. 0h boy, it was locked.

I heard a voice: "What can I do for you?" I replied, "I want to know if Dr. Imelda R. Abear is working." The locked door I could not open automatically swung, but there was nobody behind the door. I said, "Where are you?"

When I turned around, I saw behind the darkened glass window, young police and I approached & said, "I am Dr. Abear. I just want to know if my wife, Dr. Imelda R. Abear, is still working."

After he got my information, he kind of look at what appeared on a computer and said, "Yes, she is working." I felt like jumping with joy like a little child, and I answered, "Thank you, Sir!" ☺

And the door swung wide opened & like a bird out of his cage I felt like flying over the dark cloud of my problem, no longer out of mind but still out of sight where Imelda was.

When I turned at the crossroad between the Hosp and the Doctors-residences with my tunnel vision taken cared by Dr. Nguyen, the best eye doctor in the city of Ogdensburg, if not in the entire Universe, I saw the white Mercedes of Imelda parked at home.

86

Whereas I used to follow Potsie, he was now following me, running with his 4 feet trying to catch me, an old 84 yrs. But young at heart ☺. My wife knows that.

Upon arriving home, I saw she was busy cooking for our dinner. She did not ask (usually she does) where I had been. I allowed the usual event to flow silently to cover what seemed a person with schizo paranoia.

I did not ask if she came home at 6:14 PM; otherwise, I would get berated for nothing or what might appear to her, a figment of my imagination.

I just wrote in my diary on Aug. 11, 2021, because it might be significant sometime in the distant future. For one thing, she is not a figment of my imagination. My mind was not preconditioned to rule out *simbako*, schizophrenia 😄. I am a retired doctor of facts & evidence.

Similar events like this before had unfolded the explanation in the distant future. For example, when I was a lazy teenager, Brod Lading, an industrious guy who used to call me "A lazy vagabond."

It did not offend me because I could not argue against the truth, while a lie made me mad. I'm finished after years with the "Father of lies."

Anyway, one evening when I woke up from my hammock, my hideout, while Brod Lading was digging into the ground to realize his dream to create a fishpond, I found about a 9 feet scale of a passing Python underneath my hammock.

Good, I was not awakened when this Python tried to shed her old scale in view of new skin. I had no idea how to fight or flight from my hammock. I guess I was lucky.

I asked my father what it meant for the Phyton's scale she left for me & he said, "Someday, you will have a bright future." When Brod Lading heard that, he countered, "A bright future for a backbone, don't tell me?" 🤪

Anyway, for a bright future after my life of sinfulness, I decided to become a priest who loves God above all things. But after a year at the Jesuit seminary in Manila, San Jose Seminary, I was sick. Fr. Bazinet, PME, told me priesthood was not my vocation. So, I lost my "bright future." Brod Lading was right.

I am now 84 yrs., still smiling with multiple diseases going ready perhaps for a bright side of the other world where life is forever.

Brod Lading had gone gracefully long before me into that world where life is forever waiting for his Brod Elmer, "A lazy vagabond" where God might be hesitant to let poor Elmer in.

Hence, you know perhaps a little about me ☺. But don't rush either your judgment if my future is bright right now. Just judge me where Angels fear not to tread, to the former "Lazy vagabond." Oh, yay, yay 😁.

REFLECTION OF GOD, THINGS, & PERSONS

After 13 young Marines lost their lives in Afghanistan, last 8/28/21 families gathered & mourned their passing. I prayed the rosaries. We suffered the pain of the families, not so much for those who suddenly perished. Why?

Because I had experienced near-death several times, beyond pain for good people is peace of soul. Beyond pain for those who die in anger is consuming fire in Hell (Nicene Creed). Believe me or not.

You don't usually pray for those good people, RIP. In fact, we ask them to pray for us. Although I am trying to be a good man, I have more devils outside & inside me. A bad man has one or no devil because they are a devil in human form.

They kill people, except BLM, apparently supported by a bigger devil, Soros. He is not in prison because he can bail himself out quickly. Devils in human forms are usually wealthy people. Soros is Satan's price to win more souls for Hell, which would give the Devil less work. So, if you don't believe what I said, the Devil is telling you, "Don't believe Elmer."

We see devils in human forms more than Angels on TV like Fox Breaking News. Satan wants more ads on TV to let people know how rich they are (remember the island of Epstein & Clinton).

Besides most TVs, I think, don't charge them. They got a bigger audience. That is being honest especially listening to Tucker or Hannity, much more with Ingram at 10 pm with her necklace, Jesus is freely hanging on the cross.

Anyway, we rejoice with good people & we pray more for those who die in anger. Brod Lading, my Buddy, was happy at death, no more wife monkeying around; he is ok, half of my rosary.

I read from Beth's email how restless & angry her husband was at the death bed.

I think he deserves more rosaries to go into a better place. Cat wrote to me, my Sis Carmen, my most beloved Sis Inday, had a smiling face on the death bed. I guess she could not hold it; at the end of her narrow road was the golden gate opened by St. Peter, smiling.

You know, we are missionaries on earth w/o a Franciscan habit. I won't encourage you the Dominican habit. I don't know about you. I love to wear a Franciscan habit if only Emeritus, Sr. Mary Siena Bracero, will allow me.

I think she might if she will not see my scar on my shin bone. 😊 Not to mention the many scars in my soul. Confession does not remove scars of sins, even a million years in Purgatory.

Therefore, rejoice if you happen to die at the end of time because Purgatory no longer exists. Can you imagine, at the end of time, you appear before God, a 16-year-old person?

Modesty aside, I pray daily many rosaries. I don't know why: it just makes my day; otherwise, my day is blue if I cannot do so. I look forward to my small chapel to pray. God bless unless urgent my wife would leave me alone. Look who is talking to God or the devil. 😎

My wife, Imelda, does not pray as much as I do. She does not need it. She is what Christ said, "I don't come for good people (like her) because they are already saved, but I come for sinner" (Matthew 9:12).

Hence, remembering my sins, my scars remind me who am I before the eyes of God, much more so before the eyes of my former friend, the devil. Satan is no longer interested in me because my old face no longer attracts young women or old ladies older than me. I look like a 🐕 am I?

Since my devil does not qualify me for beating in the atonement of my sins (my investment afterlife) because I am not holy, I do it alone if my wife is not around. Not too often. Seldom if any.

Actually, I prefer to beat myself because I think it is less painful than Satan would do. Look at the bloody T-shirt of Padre Pio he left behind in his Monastery in Pietrelcina, Italy.

That is why Padre Pio, who had no sin, asked God if it could stop Satan from scorching him. But Padre Pio, I suppose, would add, "Not my will Lord but yours be done."

So, with pleasure, the devil continued beating Padre Pio because God allowed him to do so in reparation for the sins of the world, which until now our Lord & Mama Mary are suffering.

The irony is if people pray to Padre Pio, they get their prayers answered. But when it was Padre Pio who prayed to God, his prayer remained unanswered. Is this consistent with what Jesus said, "die to yourself (Mathew 19. 26-36)? Come and follow me".

Anyway, Padre Pio got the image & likeness of Christ crucified so he could pray & win more souls to Heaven. I do that, too, if I remember. Sometimes, forgetfulness is a blessing in old age. Don't you think so?

People with many scars of sins need more to pray; look who is talking about scars? 😊. I have a scar on my shin bone. As a little boy, I told you I chased a small girl in the dark for a lusty kiss. God protected that girl because I hit a wooden box & I failed like a monkey. She was able to escape from the small devil. 😄

I still have that scar on my shin bone. You want to see it. No charge. Donation is ok for the SAP. That is why I don't know how long I would stay, fortunately in Purgatory & not in Hell. I hope to die for my faith as a Martyr 😵 that is the holy secret to go straight to Heaven.

Remember those lions eating Christians? The bombs yesterday in Afghanistan? The reasonable 13 Marines are hopefully going to Heaven. Number 13 of every month is significant whenever Mama Mary would appear in Fatima. Don't we know Fatima was the daughter of Mohammed in the year of about 700 yrs. after Christ?

Hell must be the hardest place to stay because Jesus himself "descended into Hell & on the 3rd he rose again (3 days in Hell it did not affect him because he is God) and ascended to Heaven & seated at the right hand of his father (Nicene Creed).

That is why Jesus preached more about Hell than Heaven because many are falling into Hell every second of the day, and few are going to Heaven via Purgatory. Remember those lines when we pray daily the I BELIEVE IN GOD?

Reflection about...

THE WEDDING OF CANA

(John 2: 1-14)

Whenever I arrive in the 2nd decade of St. John Paul II's Luminous Rosary, it always reminds me of the good joke of Mo. Angelica (with some additional insight from yours truly). Proceed if this is ok with you.

When Jesus, Mary, and the five disciples arrive at the Wedding of Cana after a few minutes, the bridegroom is unaware that wine is running out. Mama Mary is embarrassed. (Who should not be if one has a normal mind)? She asks Jesus to produce some wine & Jesus says,

"O woman, what has that to do with me? My time has not yet come?" Besides the fact that Jesus called her "O woman" instead of "O Mother," it reminds us (and his mother) that he is the Messiah, the Son of God, the Emanuel among us.

I think Jesus's humility as a human being he obeyed her request. It tells us what Jesus says, "Learn from me, for I am gentle and lowly of heart (Matthew 11:29). Hence, knowing the truth, Jesus's Mom did not refute his statement, and instead, she says to the servant, "Do whatever He tells you."

Jesus says to the servant, "Fill five stone jars with water and draw some and give it to the Steward." And when the Steward tastes: it is wine and not water. So, the Steward does not know where it came from, but the servant knows.

Can you imagine? After the five fishermen, I mean, five disciples had their fill and additional best wine for them to drink? I can just imagine how they all danced, vomited, sang, and gyrated like Michael Jackson☺ in our century.

Mama Mary must have turned her face away to avoid additional, not embarrassment but shame, the kind of "friends" Jesus brought with him to the wedding of Cana.

I guess Jesus & Mary left early in order not to see the fishermen, I mean, the disciples, vomiting and falling asleep everywhere. Note: no mention in the Bible Jesus ever attended another wedding Party. ☺ Experience is indeed a great teacher. But for those who have a slow mind, Rehab is becoming a good business.

It is no wonder why very few of our Priests, after drinking wine, have become alcoholics. I am not saying drinking wine during Mass is the cause that has made them alcoholic.

Anyway, the statistics are pretty high compared nowadays in Churches or Cathedrals. Not to mention the Monasteries. *Simbako lang ipalayo sa yawa.* ☺

Neither did Jesus' fire any of the "5 fishermen" for perhaps drinking too much. With due respect to the word "Disciples" in the Bible, I thought Jesus said his time "has not yet come."

Hence, in the understanding of our present day's ceremony and verbiage, just as we changed the words, "on the 3rd day, He rose again from Hell used for centuries (The Creed) and changed it in our years to "on the 3rd day he rose from the dead."

During her telecast of the daily rosary, Mo. Angelica of the EWTN had maintained the word "Hell" while Pope Francis II had changed the word to "dead." I don't know the Apologetics if there is any distinction between using the word "Hell" and "dead."

What I know is that "on the 3rd day, He rose again from Hell and ascended into Heaven..." So, does it make it any better or worse for Jesus to stay in Hell or dead perhaps for three days when after death there is no clock in eternity?

Nevertheless, humbly I am tempted but has not fallen into to say their ordination as Disciples had not yet taken place. So, is it ok if I leave the difference or decision to you? Thank you.

THE MIND OF GOD FOR US

PROLOGUE: The door to World War III with regards to the war - Ukraine VS Putin is gaping to some but let us believe it is still closed.

Unless Putin is embarrassed that his multiple warnings meant nothing to NATO & the West would go crazy, he will put on the switch to let all his nuclear weapons fly. Where?

Of course - into Europe & the Western world except for Asia, where his buddy, the smart President of China, lived. By then, out of chaos & confusion, we face a new world order. Meanwhile, let us take a break from our current relationship with the present situation & know God's mind for us.

MONOLOGUE: Modesty aside, I recited the Holy Rosary several times a day, and in my meditation, I discovered, now late into my old age, that in the fourth joyful mystery, Joseph & Mary were stunned by what Simeon, the Prophet, said (Luke 2:32 -34) to them:

"A light for revelation to the Gentiles & for the glory for thy Israel." And Simeon added, "Behold! This child is sent for the rising and falling of many in Israel". Mama Mary did not understand this, but she kept this in her heart to ponder. Does it not tell you something?

Remember, since Simeon was a young man, he visited the Temple every day until he got very old. And yet his prayer to see Jesus, the Redeemer, was not answered. But he remained faithful to visiting God in the Temple as long as he was alive.

It appeared that Simeon must have expected to see a young man, Jesus. But instead, he saw a fragile Baby Jesus, a few months old, in his arms. The Holy Spirit must have had enlightened him "that our Redeemer Jesus was a few months old rather than a young man."

Can you imagine, rain or shine, he faithfully visited the Temple for many years? He must have had been awarded the gift of prophecy, which even Mama Mary did not have per evidence that when Simeon said to Mama Mary, I repeat,

"This child is sent for the downfall and rising of Israel." Joseph & Mary marveled to hear Simeon about this Baby Jesus. All they knew from Angel Gabriel was that he was the Son of God, named Jesus. Period.

Think for a moment: if you & I are faithful in our chosen vocations with our promise w/o being unfaithful, this is the stuff that would make you and I become a Saint.

Let us pray together to live a holy life, for nobody enters the gate of Heaven who is not a Saint. But, since most of us die with some imperfection, common sense demands the existence of Purgatory to literary wash with fire our souls before we see God in his splendor.

How lucky for those who die at the end of time if the war in Ukraine would lead us to. Purgatory no longer exists. Jesus would come "to judge the living and the dead" (I believe in God). In my humble understanding, the "living" are the faithful who are going to Heaven, and the "dead"...

Well, you know where they are going. They were a little "better" than the murderous & sinful lives they once lived while on earth. They are welcomed by Lucifer in Hell, a place Christ described where there is "gnashing & grinding of teeth," but easier for those who left their dentures on earth 😊. No teeth to grind 😁.

Anyway, Mama Mary, I repeat, was stunned to hear the prophecy of Simeon. Which meant Mama Mary was not aware of what Simeon said. I discovered that God, the Father, did not inform Mama Mary. Why?

I think God, the Father, had kept the future events of how Jesus would live so Mama Mary would not be bothered every day in her life, the anxiety of what Baby Jesus' mission to the world would be.

So that actually Mama Mary would know event by event how Jesus would spend his life to save humankind, the suffering of Jesus would gently enter the heart of Mary & Joseph. God, the Father, was apparently treating Mama Mary equally with our ordinary existence.

To some extent, I think God the Father has given us (it seemed more than Mama Mary) because we could think of what life we envision, the kind of future we would like to have. So that in our narrow road, we are filled with anxieties less we fail to serve God for his greater glory; instead, we have been doing for the greater of ourselves, don't some of us do?

Furthermore, be careful because the closer we are to Jesus and Mary, we have more devils. As I have said before, "just as Jesus earned our redemption by dying on the cross, we are living sacrificial lives to reach Heaven thru Purgatory.

And so are we in our pursuit to go to Heaven: our narrow road is laden with the vanity of earthly temptations to walk on the wide road which might lead us into temptation, but we pray, "Lord, deliver us from evil, Amen (Our Father)." Can you imagine even on the cross, Jesus was tempted for the fourth time when the devil in human form asked, "If you are the Son of God, come down from the cross?" (Luke 23:35)? This is similar to when Jesus was in retreat on the mountain. The devil asked him, "come and jump, and the Angels would catch you" (Matthew 4:5-11).

Jesus looked at the thief with love on the left side and said nothing. Might it not be surprising for Jesus, whose heart is full of divine mercy. He told us this in 1937 thru St. Faustina. Jesus could have thought, "Father, forgive him for he does not know what he is saying."

EPILOGUE: I do not know what you plan to say in your last hour on earth (usually dying in the Hosp or at home or elsewhere), unlike Jesus was tempted in his last hour (Mark 15: 33-41). You would wish to die peacefully and, if you are lucky, like Brod. Ernesto.

Yes, Brod. Ernesto, to whom our mother on earth knew the crooked life he lived called a Priest. He went to confession & Jesus in persona Christi forgave him.

He received the body of Christ. His place in the afterlife was secured, like the thief on the right side of Christ on the cross: his sins vanished like the flash of lightning, the grace he received. Brod. Ernesto, whose life I belittled & despised, please forgive me & pray for me. Alleluia!

A Personal View:

JOSEPH & MARY'S LOVE STORY

(Matthew 1:18)

At the very start, it appears incongruous to even compare the married life of Joseph and Mary to what Shakespeare had referred to as the "slings and arrows" of life to be a model of our chosen vocation towards an ideal life... why so? Because it appears like it is Heaven sent! However, it is undeniable that both Joseph and Mary were human beings just like us, who underwent the challenges of married life and came out with great success through the blessings of God.

Believe me, nothing good can come out of this world without God Almighty allowing it to happen. Pandemic, which is actually a Plague that can be likened to the time of Moses, but which is mainly a sign of our declining love for God! The Coronavirus is a murderer, wearing the crown created by Satan, which mutates with many faces, especially when we forget to love God above all things. Without God, we are Nothing!

Maybe by analyzing the narrative of Joseph and Mary's love, we can carefully consider and view how they handled the problems they encountered and, from there, learn what was really applicable in real life. These are the subtle points underlying their love for each other.

Tradition-wise, during that time, when the culture of the people was not yet far from the heart of God, it was their practice that when a woman reached the age of 16, she was bound to receive the Sacrament of Matrimony as she was presented to a group of good men.

In contrast with today's life, the young women of the Sisters of the Society of Angels of Peace (led by *Emeritus* Sr. Mary Siena Bracero;

founded by the late Msgr. Cris Espina Garcia) or other religious orders have given up their lives for a far greater vocation, to become the bride of our Lord Jesus Christ. This is a far cry from the prevailing practices in the current 21st century. Instead, we see many young men and women dating in pairs in shadowed parks, openly kissing on public beaches, or doing unimaginable sensual activities right in the midst of people.

During the time of Joseph and Mary, it was common knowledge that the good men were gainfully employed, which enabled them to raise a decent family. This practice then had practically little or no difference from a typical employment situation today. I said, "Little difference" because certain circumstances today could adversely occur, which might be considered exemptions from the currently accepted practices. These are unusual events. Many of us know, are highly probable as seen by you and me! Such exemptions could be even better known to you than I! Ha ha ha, think about it, no insult intended but did I get you thinking more deeply about such exemptions?

How did Joseph and Mary handle the challenges they faced? I think God treated them just like anyone of us, handling our conscience and our free will to choose whatever vocation we may desire. The Jesuit's motto, *"Ad majorem Dei gloriam,"* meaning "All for the greater glory of God," could be a good guide for us to follow.

It is common knowledge that the motto of Dr. Jose Rizal, author of *"Noli Me Tangere,"* offended the Spanish Government, which consequently led to his execution. Some years later, a statue was built to honor Rizal as a Hero. This was guarded by a soldier on a 24-hour shift. Why was this necessary? Perhaps the Spaniards then believed and feared that Rizal might get back to life! So, then the Spanish secret police might have to come back to kill him again, agree or disagree? heh, heh, heh.

Anyway, as we proceed to read the story of Joseph and Mary's love affair, we might also begin to understand some subtle points which could lead us to dispense some of our so-called values. In fact, these values, which we had held for a long time as basic truths, may actually be sinful acts embedded in our souls which need to be cleaned up. Particularly for Catholics, this meant going to confession, a channel whereby a Priest forgives sins in persona Christi (John 20:21) are also forgiven by God.

Through these conversations, we should be able to enrich our concept about marriage being our chosen vocation. As we move on toward the very end of our earthly lives, we will have prepared our souls for the real meaning and purpose of our existence. We seek for our new and everlasting life as promised by Christ (The Apostle's Creed) Himself. Amen.

Anyway, when Mary was presented before the eligible men she was to marry, she was already pregnant. In the light of Mary's condition and in the environment following their culture, she was, humanly speaking, a disgraced woman (most importantly, because the people were not spiritually enlightened). It was indeed a bad start for Joseph and Mary, especially when the man (Joseph) she was to marry thought she was a Virgin. Generally, young women presented before good men during their times were assumed to be Virgins. So, no one knew, except Mary, that her pregnancy was conceived by the Holy Spirit (Luke 1:27).

Mary did not tell the Religious Leader prior to the selection process because this ceremony would not have taken place if she did. Besides, if Mary had said to them that her pregnancy was conceived by the Holy Spirit (The Apostle's Creed), she would have been accused of blasphemy, and like Jesus, she too would have been crucified. So, this narrow path that Mary trod on was something she kept deep in her heart. At this point, let us take a short break and observe that...

In the 21st century, when some of us could break the "sex," I mean "the sixth commandment of God" (prior to receiving the Sacrament of Matrimony) without even showing any regret for the transgression of our modern culture simply accepts the situation. There seemed to be no remorse in connection with the man-made immorality since they are no longer bothered in view of our modern 'conscience' or way of thinking.

This is probably so because we may have lost the consciousness of decency since, perhaps due to habitual acts, our minds no longer know the difference between right and wrong. It is also possible that people no longer care to see what is right or wrong since almost everyone has accepted such practice in our society... oh, boy!

As we know, history could repeat itself, just like the incident when God's ten commandments were broken. That was exactly what Moses did! Upon seeing that the sixth commandment was broken, Moses found useless the Tablet upon which God Himself had written the ten commandments. Moses could not control himself in the face-to-face encounter where the devils appeared in human form. Unlike Pope Francis, Moses threw the Tablet, which got broken right on the face of sinners who had no more shame at all. For more details, please read the Old Testament (Exodus 20: 1-17).

It is tragic that, unlike Moses, the majority of our good people today would simply turn their heads away from the bad incident as if nothing had happened. Likewise, if we cannot change our attitude toward righteousness, civilizations like the great Roman Empire would surely deteriorate, and crimes would surge, just like what is now happening in New York City. Then everyone would surely suffer.

To date, the scenario where sins of the flesh have become rampant, even publicly displayed, and are extensively shown in movies, I-pads, cellphones, and many other forms of social media applications. In fact, some couples today do not find the need to get married. They simply live as couples without considering the serious consequence of possible pregnancy. When, by some unforeseen accident, the woman gets pregnant, very often to save face, the couple is forced to get married ready or not. Could this be a cause for laughter or perhaps pity?

In connection with the topic of marriage, divorce in the Old Testament was not part of God's original plan. Specifically, the Lord said that what "God has joined together, let no man put asunder" (Matthew 19:1-12). In this regard, "the hardness of the heart" of people during the time of

Moses, in my honest opinion, was not worse than it is in this 21st century. However, we do not only have the hardness of heart, mind & soul before God. We have also committed an unforgivable sin by the Holy Spirit mainly because "we have separated ourselves from God."

God, the Father that I love so much, you will make me happy if You allow World War III to take place today in order to end the suffering of Jesus and Mary. It had been reported from time to time that they appear to be in grave suffering in some parts of the world, where many of these sinful incidents occurred. For instance, Jesus was seen crucified before St. Francis of Assisi or Mary in tears was seen at Lourdes, France, and at Simala in Cebu, Philippines, as well as in many other places. Therefore, it is high time that we put a stop to our people's continuous hurting of our God.

Just imagine, Jesus and Mary have been suffering all these 2,000 years and perhaps yet many more years to come unless stopped earlier. Think about it, who are we to complain about our own suffering to Jesus and Mary during this pandemic when we have already enjoyed living for 90 years or less? It is even luckier for those who have lived more than a hundred years; some of them may have forgotten their own name, so when they meet face-to-face with St. Peter, he asks for their name. They cannot answer. My oh, my!

Of course, I am not saying that Jesus and Mary are always suffering. They are also happy with the few who love them, like those who die in defense of their faith and become Saints in Heaven. But these are few compared to those sinners who keep falling to hell every minute! Only God knows how many there are in this group.

I realized now what my own late Father, Juan, a holy man who knew the Bible by heart (unlike me), when he said, "Elmer, you will be happy if you will witness the end of the world." We know it will come as Jesus promised (Matthew 24: 29-31). By that time, we will have our bodies appear as if we are only 16 years old, just as Mother Mary, who was 70 years old when she died, yet appeared before the three little children in Fatima and many places like Mexico before Juan Diego as if she was only 16 years old. There is no discrimination like racism in Heaven.

As we face our judgment before God (The Creed), we present our lives the way we lived them on earth. As I mentioned in many of my published articles, if you do not believe this, just remember what St. Padre Pio said, "You will believe it when you will be there." But, by that time, there is nothing more you can do about the life you lived while still on earth. Is there a lesson here?

Now, let me continue our story about the marriage of Joseph and Mary. During those times, it was a religious practice for God to allow the people to set free a white dove (symbol of the Holy Spirit) in order to select the right husband for the lady, in this case, Mary. On the side, we may recall that in the present time, figuratively speaking, doves are actually hunted for food purposes, to be eaten just like chicken. So, for this particular occasion, the Dove sat on Joseph's head and then flew out of their sight. Perhaps it went up to Heaven. Thus officially, "Joseph became the husband of Mary (Matthew 1:18)."

We may recall that when the Angel Gabriel greeted Mary, "Hail Mary, full of grace, you have found a favor from God, and you will conceive a baby named Jesus." Mary said, "How shall this be since I have no husband?" (Luke 1:34).

After the wedding ceremony, Mary knew it was a good man Joseph, the Carpenter, who was actually their neighbor. So, I assumed, not far from where Mary lived. This was a small "city" where practically everyone knew each other.

After the ceremony, Mary and Joseph had 40 days of engagement prior to getting officially married; just like when we die, we have 40 days of engagement on earth prior to going up to Heaven for our first judgment. I said, "first judgment" because our second judgment (no exception even for Devils) can happen as we pray daily (The Apostle's Creed); we say in the last line, "the resurrection of the body and life everlasting, Amen."

Anyway, after this ceremony, Mary must have asked permission from Joseph that she was going to Judea to help Elizabeth deliver her baby, as she was already six months pregnant. Mary was at that time four months pregnant but not obviously visible.

So, after Mary helped in the delivery of Elizabeth, she came home and passed by to tell Joseph that her mission to help Elizabeth was done. Joseph must have noticed that Mary was pregnant. Their trouble had just begun. There was equity among all creatures for the flow of this event, don't you think so? Otherwise, Joseph would not have decided "to put her away quietly."

Joseph was troubled, but he did not confront Mary (the way most of us usually do while on the brink of anger and possible violence) about why she got pregnant. Joseph must be a man of great faith and not prone to rush judgment as some of us often do.

Joseph was a kind man with character, as was common during those days, but we rarely find him today. I suppose Joseph, deeply troubled for days on end, did not get an answer right away from God and perhaps said to himself, "Why did this happen to me? Have I offended God so badly that I deserve this kind of suffering?"

The best Joseph could do to protect Mary from shame (less thought of himself) was humanly speaking, I repeat, this point of frustration, was "to put her away quietly." It was at this point that Gabriel came down and told him in his dream that the baby in Mary's womb was conceived by the Holy Spirit, the promised Messiah, the son of God, named Jesus.

Not only did it amazingly bewilder and humbled Joseph, but a great burden was lifted from his broken heart, and he was prepared for a perfect love by the grace that came to Mary from God the Father Almighty. Instead of distancing himself, Joseph took her as his beloved wife. Alleluia!

POEMS

I AM AN OYSTER

I am an Oyster beneath the sea,
Below me are countless stones
Of different shapes and make up.

Today, I take a smooth stone into my heart,
I moisten her the juice of my summer love
Until she, a diamond, shines so bright.

One day a man from the earth takes her
And leaves but her darkness to me.
Below are stones, not one fits me anyway.

VERONICA

While the Apostles,
save Mary & John,
Hide in shame and
few among these
Maddening crowd of
Pharisee & Scribes
There you are Veronica,
Coming down from Calvary's hill
with your white veil.
With selfless love that
knows no fear
You move through the crack
of hardened people.
Between clenched fists and
Flogging whips I see you
gently wipe His tears away amidst cruel people.
Behind this scene Veronica,
Thanks purple veil you give to me,
I see the face of Jesus soaked
In blood and tears....
And with his sad eyes he says to me,
"Simon, do you still love me still?"

A VICTIM SOUL

Padre Pio was under siege by his Bishop for Several years.
That though he suffered much less than his
stigmata he obeyed the Pope, no more Mass for him in public.

Yet in all these years with Satan flogging on his back,
his blood drenched his white T shirt like Christ from the cross &
all the charges he received from the
Vatican it moved him not out of peace.

To thank and praise God he went
inside the Church and in locution he realized that
Christ remained hanging on the cross on behalf of his Bishop.

A PEN PAL BRIDE

At the airport a beautiful young and pretty
Maria arrived on a visitor Visa with her
Elderly American husband,
named Terry.
Some curious people from
upper Montana
Came to look at them &
felt banana.
At the cemetery, she placed a wreath
On his Terry's Dad grave when John distinctly recalled
one Summer day from Manila's slum Maria as his
Dad bride.
For an upscale Saxon family
In the heartland of North Montana
It was a disaster beyond telling
Their good neighbors
mourned that day.
Though Terry was never seen
As happier as on his wedding day
All his sons except John
had long faces:
Purple square and dry austere
Like a black rose petal in disarray.
She would abandon him no doubt.
Once she would get her
green card
And marry somewhere a
young man
Their neighbors had been
talking about.
That was 8 years ago,

John remembered,
Nothing short of tragedy happened except
One fine Spring morning
while Robins
Were chirping flying over
cherry blossoms,
Their upbeat Terry took a
heart attack
And died smiling like Elijah
in the arms of this Pregnant woman
named Maria.
Their good neighbors were banana wrong:
They wept that day &
had empathy on John
Fr. John, a Jesuit missionary
with dignity.

DECEMBER 12

I skipped to avoid her company
For my uncle was sick & dying
I must attend to his need,
But as I was about to cut
A corner & be at home at last
She appeared on the rock!

A pregnant lovely Lady dressed
In green stars studded garment:
She said, "Don't worry, he is alright Gather these
roses out of season. And give it to your Bishop that
His bud-faith may bloom all season thru."

I went to the Bishop's palace and
Handed over to him roses wrapped
In my garment & he was shocked
To see roses of different colors.
I did not know the reason why.

He took my only garment
And in excitement he forgot
To thank me or to return it.
I did not know the reason why.
Next Sunday I went to the Church
And saw my garment hanged on the wall.

Now, I knew the reason why,
Her image appeared on my garment.
Brighter than the Sun behind her.
As people bowed, they gave a dollar or two.
I knelt & offered my only two quarters
For my lunch & hungry I went home early.

THE AUGUST 15

I'm a sinful ground hog
going for a retreat into my
Winter's underground log
After I was blinded by
the swamp & C19 of Summer love.

I fast, pray, for 40 days & 40 nights
Till the break of Spring tide
Slowly I come from where I hide
Hogging my way out
From my simple monastic life:

Standing on the cherry blossom
I "see" our Lady smiling at me
As she assumes up to Heaven
Casting shadows into the abyss,
Repeat after me (she says)

"I must believe the Judge
of the living & the dead
the forgiveness of sin
the resurrection of the body"

THE URBAN HERMIT'S SONG

(For Msrg. Cris Espina Garcia)

If I keep my sins away
from the darkness in
my soul,
Then I have to constantly
Gaze beyond the blue sky.

Yet back on earth
after long hours on my knees
Once again lusty cherry blossom,
A Winter cannot hold its own,

To bury my past into oblivion
As I raise my knees
From his confessional box
The balance and the face

Of the equinox teas
simple insight
for every pain He shares with
me from the cross: He
forgives me.

A repentant sinner am I,
Christ in persona Christi have
mercy, help me to
understand your love:
I cannot give you what I do not
have.

BY THE FIRE AT LUNETA'S PARK

Our eyes that are not used to tears
Now sadly weep over the loss
If youth's unfinished dream.

We dare not see what
Jose Rizal read in nature:

He was a young lovely Moth
who burns his eager wings
by the 7 shots fired at Luneta Park

Rather than retreat into darkness
From whence he grew up.

Now standing on granite stone he is guarded 24 hrs.
a day lest he might skip as to what is happening
In his country today.

NEW YORK SUBWAY

Though he smells awful with his outfit It is his music
that perfumes my soul. In perfect symmetry his master's hand plays:
Though one string is loosed,

It's still Beethoven's symphony
Accompanied by his bare feet crafter. In New York subway
the muffled music. It creates into my whirled ears is even great.

But yet few quarters are on his plate. So I try to reach into
my pocket, someone took my wallet.
In my front pocket none much less a dime.

As I turn my back on him
I catch a glimpse of his smile.
Maybe he knows that at least,
I have tried?

MY SECOND SPRING'S LIFE

In part I of my life, I was once a young red Apple
hanging in the tree of life at the back of our house
in Ogdensburg, New York.

When I was sweet 16 and wild, I was nightly visited
by a young Bird of different feathers.
She pinned pecked me the pain and pleasure of her life,
not withstanding mine.

Now, a Savior in the order of Melchizedek took
a compassionate look at me, a lost teenage, unmasking
his covered face with 19 horns saw my soulmate
in deep atonement of my misgivings.

Transformed me by His forgiveness into an amazing,
gorgeous life, like a full-grown Rose among the weeds
and Dandelions in the Autumn of my new Second Spring's life.

THE GREEN MEADOW

In part II of my old age life, I finally fell out of grace
from the tree of life into the Green Meadow,
the Mediatrix of all graces.

Shall I say, "Too late have I found God thru no merit of my own,
but her Motherhood saved me from darkness to light!"

Now, at 84 years old I'm likened into a mere dry old Apple, a cavernous leaf,
transformed in the heart of the Green Meadow.
Gracefully, I turn into a full bloom Rose among the weeds and the
Dandelions in the Autumn of my anticipated first Spring's life.

Come my first Spring's life, on my knees, I now humbly say, "Thy kingdom come to
me thru the Mediatrix of all graces into the open gate of Heaven where my heavenly
Father reigns forever." Alleluia!

GROUNDHOG

I'm a Groundhog
When finally, my Autumn days are over go gentle into
that good night of Winter six feet below the ground.

I'm a Groundhog
stained in sinful condition,
in atonement & remorseful,
six feet under the living water of Jordan.

Till the last break of dawn
Of heavenly cherry blossoms
do I arise up into the Spring tide,
Carrying me gentle into the other side.

LOVELY LADY DRESSED IN BLUE

Teach me how to pray
For I'm a sinful ground hog
Going into my Winter retreat house
To clean the darkness of my heart,
Smeared by the swamp of Summer love.

I fast, pray, for 40 days & 40 nights.
Till the break of Spring tide
Slowly I come from where I hide
Hogging my way out
From my simple monastic life:

Standing on the cherry blossom
I see our lovely Lady dressed in blue.
Her scent turns my heart
As bright as the sun setting
Against the beauty of the West.

THE AUTUMN LEAF

(With apology, The Autumn Leaves) Dedicated to Baby May Gatchalian

Baby, I'm the Autumn leaf
Trip by the window from Haven.

And now I lay behind
The other door
Of beautiful things, remembering.

I missed your lips.
The sweet kisses of our Summer love
As I lay behind the other window of my life, longing, reminiscing.

But most of all, Baby . . .
I miss you, my darling,
As I, a golden leaf, God willing,
I'm on my way to Heaven.

THE FUNERAL OF ADAM & EVE

It is easy to choose evil over good.
But the passing pleasure it offers
Is a lifetime of atonement to forget.

Truly, it is hard to choose good over evil.
But the result it gives us peace of mind and soul.
No one can take it away from us except ourselves.

Adam and Eve are not the reason for this.
It appears they are only subjective for our reason to be.
We apparently do not inherit sin.

When we can choose to make our own Favorite sin.
It is not fair either Adam or Eve to blame.
It is silly.

Over the quintessence of love's free will is
God's gift for us to choose between good and evil.
It is by this choice what everlasting life we will worthily live.
Amen.

DAVID BLOOM – TILL THE LAST WOLF

(In honor of Mr. David Bloom who died in Iraq, 3/2002)

Under confusing ideological wind
In Iraq David Bloom came
As a hunter would protect
The freedom of his sheep.

In the dark field where
Roving wolves stand fast
The heat, the cold, the sandstorm
Somehow took a heavy toll on him.

As he searched for the truth
To tell us about the endless war
In Iraq where freedom lays bare
At the mercy of these faceless wolves.

Beyond now David Bloom is gone.
But our screaming Eagles
Shall track down their footprints
Till the last wolf is accounted for
And freedom is at last won.

VERSES OF OUR FATHER'S LOVE

We have realized from the years passed about the care and love you've given us.

Once, we were infants, sick and crying thru the night you called a doctor. And we cried more when his big needle sank deep into our bums. You stayed to comfort us, and we rewarded you a sleepless night and swampy diapers beside our wailing bed.

When we were children and did wrong you never spared the rod. And yet, like me, not all branches were growing straight:

But nobody could do better than what you did, "Whack, whip, whack, Oh! boy," I said to myself, "I won't do that foolishness again; but a little later I said, "not yet."

Then, World War II broke and you hid us (like a castrated Roster under his wings to protect us from the brown chick-eating hawk) in Kansuji beyond the touch of broken brothers across the whole world who cut themselves in darkness.

The War had taken the best in us. We had to leave Argao across the sea to Mindanao, the land of promise, where in Davao the coconuts were young, and the pasture was green. We hoped for a better tomorrow to come.

And yet later, amidst the laugher and success that Binugao in Davao City had given us, we got lost in the rainbow that was not in our own making but yours and Mama. How ingratitude became part of our vocabulary in our brains.

These were the times that in our modest wealth, our family was lost and was shaken by madness to its root: we wanted this; we wanted that. Our greed, "hook line & sinker", became the bait we took unto ourselves. We knew no respect.

With all these misunderstandings you stood like an Oak tree, with kindness with strength and compassion with love that was almost Christlike and so we endured.

Indeed, you did not only show us not generally in words but by your unlimited examples of patience and sacrifices, the way how to live on the narrow road of life which eventually by the grace of God thru Mama Mary had obtained for us, peace and love in our souls.

So, forgive us for our "wisdom" that fell short of what was beyond the horizon of your foresight.

Now, you are old, shrunk, bald headed but not a symbol of weaknesses but of strength that had silent so many storms in the sea of life and shoved us off into the coastal shore of Binugao, Davao.

Pope Paul VI rewarded you in 1964 as one of the ten most outstanding families throughout the Philippines.

Indeed, we are proud to pass this honor to our next generation. That none of us fail for our Father's sake, so God help us.

A WOLF

I'm a Wolf
Barking at the full moon at night,
Never "it" falls from Heaven
No matter how I thirst from my cross

Where people
with the same brand of mine
thrive for a holy living
Barking at the full moon at night.

I'm a Wolf
I find a Lamp & eat his hide;
he offers me his blood to drink
And that makes all the difference!!

HERE IN AMERICA

Here in America,
I missed the joy of poverty
In my country.

I see people with small head
With big stomach
Waggling on the wide road
of leftist agenda.

Here at home
I missed people, with big head, thin
Tummy walking on the narrow road,
Some arriving Heaven thru Purgatory.

Here in America,
I see a big Camel trying hopelessly
To enter thru a small eye
of a needle.

Here at home
I missed to see a wider eye of a needle
Easy for a camel to get thru
To enter the gate of Heaven.

Yet, here in America
I draw myself closer to God
Trying to make up what I missed at home.

FROM A DARK CAVE

At last, Nardo captured this snake:
Fatso, after devouring his chick.
Into the bamboo cage she was kept.
Except for the Chinese cuisine.
This snake was good for nothing.

To increase his profit.
He served her a fat chick
Days draining by her head
She didn't eat, "Eat or you die snake,"

Nardo said. But she appeared dead
And Nardo laughed for he knew
She was playing dead.
For just yesterday she was so alert

When his fighting roster peeked
On her between the bamboo slots
And how she looked at his roster
Askew-mad with a retraining fire.

Weeks went by she lost so much
Weight she was able to slip
And "Oh my God!" he found
His favorite fighting rooster dead

A slow hurricane 4 of anger
Was raging inside his head
He went into her hiding place,
And set the dark cave Ablaze

A week after he lost another
Of his best fighting rooster
And Nardo was mad, very mad.

BLACK MOUSE

A Black Mouse
A small change his son's path
Was enough to aflame his dad's heart
Sending black smoke into his head
Which housed a black mouse Hard as a rock
A little excuse for such change
In mood could not trivialize
The situation inside his head
But only kept his black
Mouse ablaze
And before this rock
would break by his ritual toil
He left his dad
In his droughty house
Like an old mental dog
Licking his bleeding paws
After mauling a stuff black mouse
That won't not go away
In the cul-de-sac of his own mind

Note: The black mouse is the Metaphor of an obsessive-compulsive mind. A kind of person who for example keeps checking the door of his house at night whether it is locked or not and won't stop until the poor door gives way, and his wife is up!

A CANDLE FIRE

As a young man you discover
For yourself a late autumn rose
In her out of springtime
This spooky chilly summer night
Under the beauty of fading Stars.
Yes, under the beauty
Of waning but immortal
Stars.

One Shadow is enough
to warm this cozy night
And make a candle fire
For this solitary 14th
moon to shine
in late summer day
When this, out of spring
Rose.

Shod in her cursed slippers
Would be seen dancing
Would be seen dancing
Away her old petals in lieu
Of her new spring Down
Bud.

HOSPITAL

To keep the scabs out
I saw Dad and Mom at home
Often chasing at each
Other's throat

For lack of money and attention
While I sat disconnected cow
Munching a leftover bean,
A bunch of yuck

And so, one day
While I was next door playing
I saw Mom left Dad for another man.
Near St. Lawrence River,
Far, far back door.

Dad shouted at my face,
"I warn you, no more eating next door, Okay?"
But this morning
Across my neighbor's Limousine
Dad saw me eating.

Angry, beckoned me to come,
His jaw-muscles moved like worm
Underneath his haggard
Cheekbones.

"How could you do this to me
When your father's friends
have put us down!"
He shouted beyond my ears.

Shaking he came nearer
But before he could hold
My throat I ran like a dog
With a shrunken tail between my legs.

And glancing back I saw.
A madman, sporting a T-shirt: "Scabs, Keep out!
I am on strike."
Panting, I arrived in another house
Near St. Lawrence River.
Far, far back door.

SCABS

"*Scabs Keep out!*"
Ever since Dad was on strike
In front of Claxton-Hepburn
Hospital. To keep the scabs out
Things had changed at home.

Where once we lived
In a world of make believe
My Birthdays brought me Gift
Beyond my Belief

Dad and Mom were often chasing
For a kiss across table full of goods,
While I sat contented cow munching
My favorite cookies often with my friend,

Rita who lived near St. Lawrence River
Far, far back door.
But ever since Dad was on strike
In front of Claxton-Hepburn

AN INSCAPE AT SYLVIAN'S LAKE

I left my bicycle in Argao to rot.
Now I'm facing the frozen ice of Alberta's Sylvian lake like
a curious out of town Rat.

I walked on the frozen
from the shore yet the ice cracked
every time I stepped forward.

Scared I might sink & be frozen alive
I turned around but every step
I did the ice cracked.

I run with my remaining life.
Thanks God! I reached beyond
the red shoreline:

Two lessons I learnt, fast & slow:
First, if you love someone 'nga matipid,'
Try to crack the frozen lake inside her head.

Believe me I tried someone I love:
She returned with her head, cracked,
Leaking her charity into my heart!

Second, I saw the cracked white ice ashore:
dressed in white but there is sacrificial
death underneath the shadow of our Savior's life.

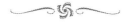

THE 'WHITE' FROZEN OF QUIDI VIDI LAKE

It was the edge of Winter in 1978
When I arrived at Newfoundland
from Cebu, a Philippine's Island

That I found myself alone facing
the 'white' frozen of Quidi Vidi Lake.
Why were no people skating?

The beauty of the frozen Lake
lighted by the morning sunlight
with Turtle doves on flight,

Tempted me out of mind & foresight.
I walked on the 'white' ice, but it cracked
For every step I did & be frozen underneath

I run back like an old bird on flight
But the ice cracked every step I made.
I flew faster with underrunning fright.

Thanks God, I reached the shoreline.
My wife asked why I ventured into a lake
Dressed in white but death underneath!

I TO DISCOVER THIS...

Thank you, my son,
what you discovered on earth and
If I dare to say, you are my son as well from
Grave to Heaven.

On the spot is I say,
one constant line
is a reminder, a guide
for what is the right way,

"Soe, you & I,
live a borrowed life,
When your life is over & done
You return it to Someone.

And in return he gives you
an everlasting life.
The strange thing is he owes you
nothing you cannot describe

Because he is everything.
He has no life because he is life.
He has no love because he is love.
So do not fail him

Because you cannot give him
What you do not have
what life & love
you & I owe from him.

MY ADDRESS TO YOU

I luv the full moon at night
Though alone with blue strawberry fire.
Flirting among changing stars out of sight.

Lord, am I not in luv like a flying Bat?
At the sight of Eve's red apple face.
Sweet sour beauty valor and act?

Yes, I go gentle into a goodnight risking disobedience as
I kiss her face.
Where all of you have begun.

WHAT THE READERS SAY

"It's everyone's wish to enter the Gate of Heaven after our earthly life and it's up to our Creator in heaven to decide for that when the judgement comes.

Thank you Tio for your thoughts and wisdom and it makes us realize to do good while we are still here on earth and not to be fascinated by material things. Stay safe and blessed!"

Walter A. Abear, MD.

WHAT THE READERS SAY

"After read your article so nice. Para kanako you did enjoy your lovelife when you were at their age hihi. Like ours also hihi. Mau bitaw uncle when God gives us joyful moments ato gyud tagamtamon kay dili na gyud mubalik same incidents. Ang bahandi makita apan ang oras dili na mubalik.

During this pandemic, I realized dako kaayo katabang ning mga pictures kay katon dili na ta kalaag laag. So with this, it takes us back in time. Maayo na lang cle sige mi laag laag sa dihang naa pay kwarta hihi ang mga nawong gwapo ug gwapa. Diha pay picture namo sa cansuje nga arang pagkaninduta hihihi.

Maayo gani uncle kay mag 50 na mo kami katunga pa unya ang kalibutan karon daghan nang panghitabo. Daghan uncertainties.

Uncle we are praying that time would be good to you. Makauli mo pinas for your golden wedding."

Bebot Pingol Tan

WHAT THE READERS SAY

"Reading your book, "Profile of Love" I found it interesting and heartwarming. It's not only interesting true to life experiences but profound & humorous as well.

Having the chance to read it, is a chance worth to treasure of. Every message he shared is worth to ponder & meditate.

As I remembered one of the thoughts that reminded me "Keeping in Touch with God I am here on earth for just a little while" it reminded me that we are just temporary in this world of make believe.

The highest form of prayer is when we sing our prayers like every high Mass and so as the rhythm of these poems in this book would uplift our hearts if we sing while reading, Alleluia!"

Jobelle A. Payumo, BS, Math

WHAT THE READERS SAY

"I enjoyed your story, giving me insight of your life many, many years ago. If I may say so, I think those days were considerably better to live in, than the current times.

There was no climate change then & certainly no COVID-19 pandemic. I wish my grandchildren could experience those days. So different from this age of modern technology.

Certainly, the good Lord has been kind to you and Tia Mel, blessing you with long life & loving family. You have been blessed because I know you have been a blessing to others, too.
Spread your blessings around and it comes back to you a hundred-fold. You are a perfect example of that.

My prayer for you is that may you continue to be God's instrument of spreading his word through your writings & lifestyle.

Rolly and I sincerely wish you both live longer healthy lives spent with the people you most hold dear."

Arhlene & Rolly Bachilier

ABOUT THE AUTHORS

Elmer M. Abear, M.D. was a Jesuit seminarian at San Jose Seminary, Philippines in 1978; Consultant Editor, Escolapion, Cebu Institute of Medicine in 1970; Literary Editor-in-Chief, Southwestern University's school organ in 1966; Editor in Chief, Mindanao Collegian, Mindanao University, graduated, A.B. in 1969; English Professor, St. Michael's College, Philippines; 3rd Degree Member of Knights of Columbus. Author of 4 books. Married to Dr. Imelda Ramirez in 1972 and has 3 children: Rossana, Butch and Dave.

Cesar Abear, AB. (SOE) spent 26 years in detailing and promoting pharmaceutical products for Zuellig, Parke Davis, and Bayer in the Philippines. Retired as a National Sales Manager. A Roman Catholic in faith. Member, Knights of Columbus. Currently lives in California, USA with wife, Abeth Lavina, daughter Mary Grace, and grandchildren – Alton and Alette. He has other two sons, Ton, and Mao. Mao and his wife, Debbie has 3 children, Alyanna, Alex, and Aiden.

ABOUT THE ARTIST

Alton Abear, is an aspiring graphic artist and musician. At a very young age, he has shown great interest in expressive arts by drawing his imagination and showcasing his creativity using different art mediums. He communicates best through his art. Through the years, he has broadened his artistic skills by engaging in painting and graphic sketching. Nowadays, he is involved in music by composing and recording covers of his favorite music artists.

ABOUT THE EDITOR

Tonette Abear, MS, is the grandniece of Elmer and Imelda. She is currently completing her doctoral internship in Psychology at the University of California.

BIBLIOGRAPHY

Published Books: 1980-2008
Life in Newfoundland, published, Newfoundland Writers.
I am Therefore I Think, published, Minerva Press, U.K.
The Life & Joy of Rossana, Philippines Press
The Passion of Christ, published, Trafford, Ontario, Canada
GONE, published, Tate Publishing & Enterprise, U.S.A.
Second Spring part I, published, Legauia, U.S.A.

Second Spring part III, Too Late have I Found God, published, Philippines Press

Unpublished Booklets, 110 - 120 pages each.
(For publication in case of generous sponsors)
Second Spring part IV
Second Spring part V
Second Spring part VI
Second Spring part VII
by Minerva Publishing House

>>>> **END** <<<<